Arkansas

ARKANSAS BY ROAD

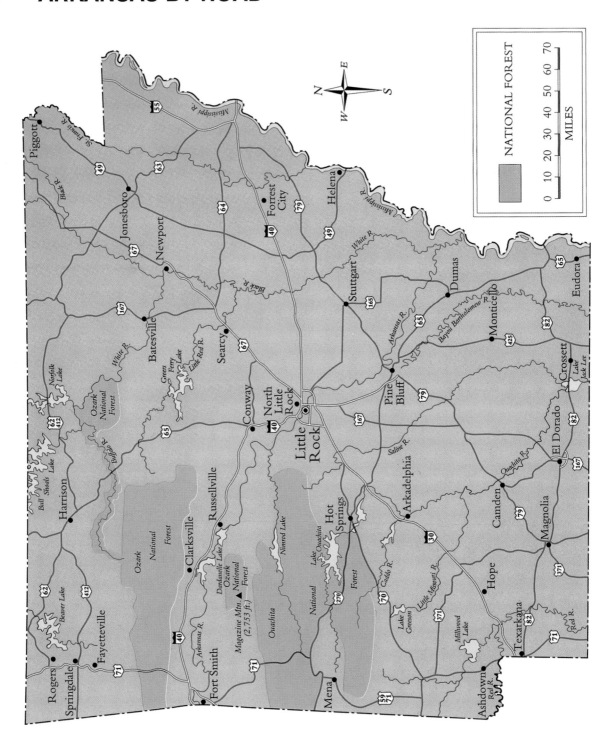

Celebrate the States

Arkansas

Linda Jacobs Altman, Ettagale Blauer, and Jason Lauré

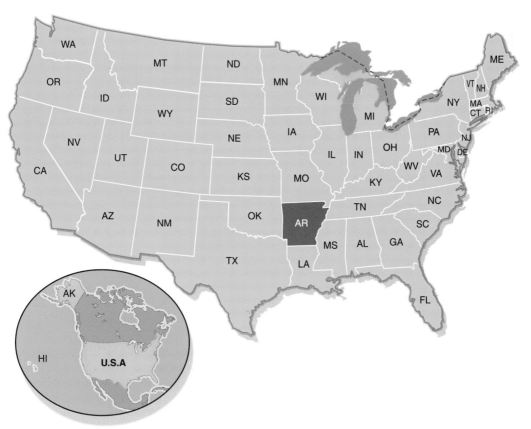

Marshall Cavendish
Benchmark
New York

Marshall Cavendish Benchmark
99 White Plains Road
Tarrytown, New York 10591-5502
www.marshallcavendish.us

All Internet sites were correct at time of printing.

Library of Congress Cataloging-in-Publication Data
Altman, Linda Jacobs, 1943-
Arkansas / by Linda Jacobs Altman, Ettagale Blauer, and Jason Lauré. — 2nd ed.
p. cm. — (Celebrate the states)
Summary: "Provides comprehensive information on the geography, history, wildlife, governmental
structure, economy, cultural diversity, peoples, religion, and landmarks of
Arkansas"—Provided by publisher.
Includes bibliographical references and index.
ISBN 978-0-7614-3001-8
1. Arkansas—Juvenile literature. I. Blauer, Ettagale. II. Lauré, Jason. III. Title.
F411.3.A48 2008
976.7—dc22
2007036798

Editor: Christine Florie
Contributing Editor: Nikki Bruno Clapper
Publisher: Michelle Bisson
Art Director: Anahid Hamparian
Series Designer: Adam Mietlowski

Photo research by Connie Gardner

Cover photo by Ryan Beyer/Getty Images

The photographs in this book are used by permission and through the courtesy of: *Corbis:* Tim
Thompson, back cover, 14, 99, 105; John Wigman, 16; Buddy Mays, 23, 24(B), 66, 94; Carl and Ann
Purcell, 29, 82, 104; George D. Lepp, 30; CORBIS, 43; Bettmann, 46, 47, 49, 123; Dorothea Lange,
48; Irwin Thompson, 55, 59, 61, 63; Kim Kulish, 73; JP Laffont, 77; Bill Barksdale, 84; Greg Smith,
91; Bob Krist, 106, 135; Ralph A. Clevenger, 111(B); W. Perry Conway, 114; Andy Willsher, 126; Rick
Friedman, 127; *Danita Delimont:* Gayle Harper, 8; David Frazier, 87, 92; *Alamy:* Classic Stock, 12;
North Wind Picture Archives, 33; Chad Shahar, 45; Wesley Hitt, 90; Don Smetzer, 103; *Getty Images:*
Harrison Shull, 13; Scott Olsen, 21; Francis Miller Stringer, 51; Matt Carr, 56; Chris Cheadle, 111(T);
Hulton Archive, 130; Randy Belice, 131; *Digital Rail Road:* Bill Parsons, 68; *The Image Works:* Mary
Evans Picture Library, 32; David Frazier, 54; Jeff Greenberg, 65; Richard Lord, 69; Syracuse Newspa-
pers/Frank Ordonez, 122; Topham, 129; *North Wind Picture Archive:* 34, 100; *Art Resource:* Smithsonian
American Art Museum/Washington DC, U.S.A.; *Gibson Stock Photography:* 52; *Super Stock:* Richard
Cummins, 74; age footstock, 98; *Dembinsky Photo Associates:* Terry Donnelly, 17, 18, 19, 108; *Minden
Pictures:* David Tipling, 24(T); Tim Fitzharris, 25; *Arkansas Gazette,* 39; *Animals/Animals:* Fred
Whitehead, 26; *Photo Researchers:* Tom McHugh, 27; Dante Fenolio, 28.

Printed in Malaysia
1 3 5 6 4 2

Contents

Arkansas Is . . .

Arkansas is a peaceful place . . .

"There's a feeling . . . of being a million miles away from New York instead of a mere three-and-a-half-hour plane ride. There doesn't seem to be a rush about much of anything. The air is clean and the hills are so lovely that you want to imprint their beauty in your mind for mental vacations the rest of the year."

—journalist Carla Sanders

. . . whose people remember their history.

"'Daisy, they're here! The soldiers are here! Aren't you excited? Aren't you happy?' a reporter asked. Any time it takes eleven thousand five hundred soldiers to assure nine Negro children their constitutional right in a democratic society, I can't be happy."

—NAACP official Daisy Bates at Central High School, regarding the school's racial integration with the help of National Guard troops

Arkansans have a rich culture . . .

"If I could rest anywhere, it would be in Arkansas, where the men are of the real half-horse, half-alligator breed such as grows nowhere else on the face of the universal earth."

—Davy Crockett

"I have a passion that people should understand agriculture. When 2 percent of Americans produce food and fiber for the world, I feel it's important that people understand us."

—Susan Anglin, farmer in Benton County

. . . and aren't afraid to show a sense of humor . . .

"Arkansas must be a whole lot older than folks think; it's even mentioned in the Bible. Right there in Genesis it says, 'Noah looked out of the ark and saw.'"

—anonymous

"Legend has it that Ink, Arkansas, was named by postal officials who filled in a form which asked for the town's new name. The instructions said 'write in ink,' and so they did."

—writers Ken Beck and Terry Beck

. . . and take patriotism seriously.

"On Memorial Day [2004], the state of Arkansas mourns the loss of nine Arkansas National Guard soldiers killed in Iraq since their arrival in April [2003]. The Arkansas National Guard now has the highest casualty rate of any National Guard brigade in the country."

—diary entry from "Off to War" on the Discovery Channel

Arkansas is one of the best-kept secrets in the United States. Arkansas is home to Hot Springs, the first national park in the country, and is packed with fifty-one other state parks. Its varied terrain and natural beauty, spread across 150,000 acres of wilderness, attract visitors throughout the year. There are hundreds of campgrounds, hiking trails, streams, and caverns to explore. Even a short visit to Arkansas explains the state's nickname, the Natural State. However, it is also a thriving, modern state with vibrant cities, arts programs, and major universities such as the University of Arkansas. While people in the Mississippi Delta region experience high rates of poverty and unemployment, most of the other regions are experiencing tremendous growth and prosperity. There is a feeling that Arkansas is definitely on the way up.

Chapter One

A Good and Pleasant Land

Arkansas's roots lie in the traditions and cultures of the South. Its varied landscapes, as well as the varied lifestyles of its residents, shape the state. First-time visitors find the beauty of Arkansas a delightful surprise. The courtesy and friendliness of Arkansans also makes a visit there a charming experience.

Roughly square in shape, Arkansas is bounded by Missouri to the north, Tennessee and Mississippi to the east, Louisiana to the south, Oklahoma to the west, and Texas at its southwest corner. The entire eastern border is formed by the Mississippi River.

There is a strange notch missing from the northeastern corner of the state. It looks like someone carefully cut out a small piece of Arkansas and left it in Missouri. That is just about what happened. When Arkansas's border was being set in 1819, a wealthy landowner named

Arkansas has an astonishing diversity of landscapes. The Buffalo National River, pictured here, is protected by the U.S. government.

LAND AND WATER

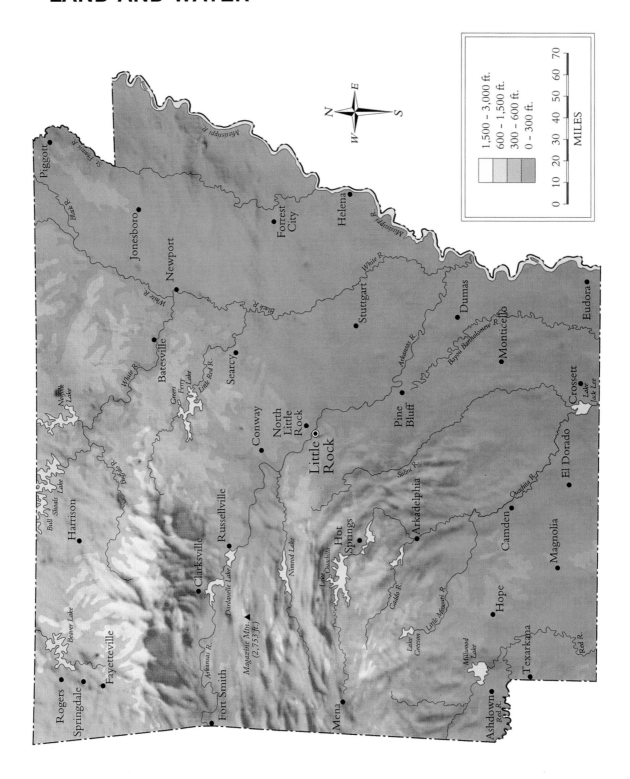

Colonel John H. Walker didn't want his holdings split between two states. Friends in high places made sure that Colonel Walker's property ended up on the Missouri side. This is how Arkansas ended up with a notch.

LANDFORMS

Arkansas's landscape varies dramatically, from the green grandeur of the Ozark Mountains to the steamy Mississippi Delta country. It is divided almost equally between highlands in the northwest and lowlands in the southeast.

The Highland Region

The highland region includes the Ozark Plateau, the Ouachita (pronounced WA-sheh-taw) Mountains, and the Arkansas River Valley, which separates the plateau from the mountains. The word *Ozark* comes from the French *aux arcs*, which means "at the bows." Nobody seems to know exactly how this name applies. Some say it could refer to the curves and bends in the mountains' rivers and trails, or perhaps it refers to the archery bows of Native Americans.

Whatever the origin of the name, the Ozarks are widely regarded as one of the most beautiful areas in the United States. Rugged hills, dotted with caves and sinkholes, rise to the peaks of the Boston Mountains, more than 2,000 feet above sea level. After a hike through the Ozarks, backpacker Dennis Thomas said the mountains "look suspiciously like a picture-perfect postcard."

The Ozarks are made up of hollows and knobs. Hollows—or hollers, as the hill folk call them—are deep, narrow valleys carved over countless thousands of years by fast-moving rivers and streams. Knobs are hills with noticeably rounded tops. For newcomer Elliott West, these hills and valleys are a natural paradise: "There are dogwoods, huckleberries, and uncountable

Whitaker Point is located in the Upper Buffalo Wilderness section of the Ozark National Forest.

wildflowers, creeks, and caves. . . . We can hike for hours, seeing no other people but plenty of hawks . . . woodpeckers, and deer, with occasional wild turkeys, skunks, armadillos, foxes, porcupines. . . . It is a varied landscape, one we will spend our lives getting to know."

A climber scales Magazine Mountain, the highest peak in Arkansas.

The Arkansas River Valley is a wide trough cut by the ceaseless motion of the river. Near the riverbanks, the land is fairly level and suitable for farming. Here and there, a lone mountain interrupts the level terrain. Arkansas's tallest peak, Magazine Mountain, rises from this valley.

The Arkansas River Valley is bordered on the south by the Ouachita Mountains. Their name comes from a Native-American word meaning "good hunting grounds." The Ouachitas are a series of ridges and ravines running in an east-west direction.

The Lowland Region

The Arkansas lowlands include the Gulf Coastal Plain in the south and the Mississippi Delta in the east. A third division, Crowley's Ridge, cuts like a jagged scar across the delta.

The Gulf Coastal Plain extends from the Gulf of Mexico into southwestern Arkansas. Dense forests of pine once grew wild on the rolling plain. Today, commercial timber companies plant and manage the forests. Trees thrive in the sandy clay soil.

Bayou Bartholomew is a peaceful, beautiful part of the Mississippi Delta.

In the southern part of the Mississippi Delta lies Bayou Bartholomew, partly in Arkansas but mostly in neighboring Louisiana. A bayou is a shallow, curving channel filled with slow-moving or stagnant water. Bartholomew is believed to be the longest bayou in the world. Because the soil is never dry, water-loving grasses, bushes, and trees grow everywhere. Sometimes, in the heat, fog rises from the surface. Then the bayou becomes a place of mystery, silent except for animal noises: the croaking of armies of frogs, the calls of passing birds, and the splashing of an alligator as it slips into a stream.

A major conservation effort to restore Bayou Bartholomew began in 1995. Dr. Curtis Merrell formed an alliance when he gathered a group of concerned local landowners to help improve the water in the bayou. They had a very big job ahead of them. The channel was used as an illegal dumping site where people tossed their old furniture, cars, farm machinery, and garbage.

Farming the land along the bayou's banks led to the loss of plants and trees that normally hold the soil together. Soil erosion led to a loss of habitat for fish and other wildlife. All of these problems had to be addressed with an overall plan that would preserve the bayou's water quality while improving the habitat for wildlife. Once the environment improved, the region would be suitable for responsible fishing and recreational activities.

Improvements to the bayou have been promising. The alliance has provided nearly 1.75 million hardwood tree seedlings to landowners. The numbers of fish and other species have grown significantly since 1995. College students from around the region help to monitor the fish population. By 2007, the bayou was home to more than 117 species of fish, including the particularly valuable largemouth and spotted bass. Other volunteers have worked to remove 169 tons of trash from Bayou Bartholomew. Hundreds of Boy Scouts have earned environmental science merit badges for their work on the bayou.

The Mississippi Delta covers the eastern third of Arkansas, from the Louisiana border all the way up to Missouri. The delta's rich soil, which is deposited by the flooding of the Mississippi River, is the best farmland in Arkansas. Rice, soybeans, cotton, and many other crops grow on the flat, fertile land. Crowley's Ridge is perhaps the oddest landform in Arkansas. It is 200 feet high, 200 miles long, and so narrow that it appears as a startling interruption to the delta lowlands. This densely forested ridge is covered with a pale yellow, powdery substance called loess.

A cotton grower inspects his crop in the Mississippi Delta region.

WATERWAYS

Two major rivers help shape the life of Arkansas. The mighty Mississippi River forms Arkansas's eastern border, except for the notch in the northeastern corner. This river nourishes the soil in the delta region. The second major river, the Arkansas, flows through the highland valley that shares its name. It passes through the capital city, Little Rock, on its way across the state and joins the Mississippi River. Other important rivers are the White River in the northeast, the Ouachita River in the west, and the Red River, which forms part of Arkansas's border with Texas.

The Petit Jean Mountain overlook provides a lovely view of the Arkansas River.

Arkansas also has a wealth of streams. Many have colorful names such as Strawberry, Crooked Creek, War Eagle, and Big Piney. Streams are not as wide or as deep as larger rivers, and they do not cover as much territory. Because their water rushes through narrow channels, streams do not move with the stately grandeur of big rivers. Instead, they usually flow quickly, and in steep, mountainous terrain they crash, dash, and explode into great white-water froths.

The Buffalo National River in the Ozarks was the first stream placed under federal government protection. This beautiful 150-mile-long stream plunges down 2,000 feet of mountainside, through limestone bluffs and dense forests, and joins the White River.

Water cascades dramatically in Lost Canyon on the Buffalo National River.

Arkansas is famous for its natural springs. Springs are water sources that bubble up from the earth. Many people believe that the minerals in spring water improve their health. The headwaters of the Spring River are at Mammoth Spring, one of the largest springs in the world. Nearly 10 million gallons of water flow out of Mammoth Spring every hour. There are several hot mineral springs in the Ouachita Mountains. The best known is Hot Springs, where there are forty-seven naturally heated springs. The waters are used for drinking and bathing.

Boiling Springs is one of many natural water sources in Hot Springs National Park.

Arkansas has many lakes, both natural and artificial. Lake Chicot in the Mississippi Delta is the largest natural lake in the state. It is an oxbow lake, a type of lake that was originally a sharp bend in a river, but was cut off when the river changed course. Most artificial lakes in Arkansas were created when people dammed rivers. The state's dams provide water storage, control flooding, and generate hydroelectric power. Among the state's important artificial lakes are Lake Ouachita and Lake Catherine on the Ouachita River, Dardanelle Lake on the Arkansas River, and Beaver Lake on the White River.

THE CLIMATE

Arkansas has a warm and humid climate. Statewide, the average temperature is 82 degrees Fahrenheit in July and 45 °F in January. In Arkansas, there is highland weather and there is lowland weather. Each region has its own patterns.

The northern highlands average about 40 inches of rain each year. March through May is the wettest period. Winter brings 20 °F temperatures and a dusting of snow to the Ozarks. In autumn, the leaves turn to shades of copper, crimson, and golden yellow.

The southern lowlands receive an average of 55 inches of rain per year. In this region, December and January are the wettest months. Winters in southern Arkansas are milder and shorter than those in the north. Summers are hot and humid—temperatures can soar into the nineties, and the moisture in the air makes it feel even hotter. "July in the delta starts feeling like you could grab a handful of air and wring it out like an old waterlogged dishrag," said one Arkansan.

In 2007, Arkansas, along with much of the southeastern United States, suffered a prolonged drought marked by periods of 100-plus-degree days.

At least four people died. Much of the state was under a fire watch, and people were warned not to light fires for barbecues or to burn brush during this period. Farming communities whose crops were stunted faced long-term effects of the drought.

TORNADO ALLEY

Like its neighboring states, Arkansas lies in a region known as Tornado Alley. This nickname reflects a rather tragic fact: tornados—whirling, violent windstorms—sweep across the land in early spring as cold weather gives way to warm weather. Tornadoes are unpredictable and extremely destructive. In a matter of minutes, an entire town can be wiped off the map. From 1997 to 2006, Arkansas was the state that suffered the most violent tornadoes. In this time period, there were thirty-four such windstorms in the state. Twenty-eight were in the F3 category, and six were in the F4 category. (F5 is the category of the most powerful tornadoes.)

A tornado overturns vehicles in Marmaduke in April 2006.

During the period from April 1 to April 3, 2006, seven counties of Arkansas were hit hard. The tornadoes seemed to skip all around, hitting counties in the north and center of the state but sparing other areas. When Governor Mike Huckabee toured the region immediately afterward, he declared disaster areas in Cross, Fulton, Greene, Randolph, and White counties. Two other counties, Conway and Hot Spring, already had been declared disaster areas. Roofs were ripped off some buildings, while other buildings were completely flattened.

In early February 2008 tornadoes raged through Arkansas as a result of severe weather. Thirteen people in four counties were killed.

PLANTS AND ANIMALS

Arkansas is rich with wild plants. More than half the state is forested. Hardwoods such as ash, hickory, maple, and oak grow in the northern part of the state. In the southwest there are softwood forests, which contain mostly loblolly and shortleaf pine. Flowering tulip trees, also known as yellow poplars, grow on Crowley's Ridge.

Other flowering trees and shrubs include dogwood, redbud, and azalea. In springtime, the trees blossom and wildflowers carpet meadows, hillsides, and riverbanks. Arkansas has bluebells, hydrangeas, Indian blankets, water lilies, and sweet-smelling yellow jasmine. The lady's slipper, a species of wild orchid, grows in the pine forests of the Gulf Coastal Plain.

A redbud tree adds color to the Ozark Mountains.

Golden Indian blanket flowers thrive in the Ouachita Mountains.

Arkansas has many species of birds, including robins, mockingbirds, phoebes, and cardinals. The distinctive call of the whippoorwill often sounds in the Ozark night.

Fish such as bass, catfish, and perch populate Arkansas's lakes and streams. Lobsterlike crawfish, also called crawdads or mudbugs, are abundant in the Mississippi Delta. Arkansas also has its share of reptiles and amphibians. The green anole lizard, for example, can be found in the forests of the Ouachita Mountains.

The mockingbird has been named Arkansas's official state bird.

A green anole lizard rests on a mushroom in the Ouachita National Forest.

Among the state's forest animals are raccoons, skunks, weasels, woodchucks, foxes, rabbits, and deer. The animal most closely associated with Arkansas is probably the razorback hog. This wild boar, described by one Arkansan as "a couple hundred pounds of mean and ugly, with bristles down its back," is the University of Arkansas mascot. When Razorback fans cheer their sports teams, they use an old-time Arkansas hog call: "Woo, Pig, Souie! Woo, Pig, Souie! Woo, Pig, Souie! Razorbacks!"

Skunks can be found throughout the state.

The razorback hog is part of both the wildlife and the culture of Arkansas.

DID YOU SEE THAT BIRD?

In 2005, John Fitzpatrick, from the Cornell Lab of Ornithology, announced that a team of bird-watchers had spotted an ivory-billed woodpecker, a bird that had been seen last along the Bayou De View in 1944. This was very big news in the bird-watching world. But was the bird really spotted?

Teams later tried to duplicate the spotting somewhere in a half-million-acre region near the White River. They failed to find even a feather. Whether the sighting was genuine or mistaken, however, it drew worldwide attention both to the woodpecker and to the beautiful woods and wetlands of Arkansas.

Scientists are hoping to prove that the ivory-billed woodpecker still exists. Pictured here is a museum specimen.

BATS!

Arkansas is home to three species of endangered bats: the Ozark big-eared bat, the gray bat, and the Indiana bat.

Ozark big-eared bats are well named: their ears are huge, their faces comically fierce. Only about three hundred Ozark big-eareds remain in Arkansas. They live in two Ozark caves—they hibernate in one and have babies in the other. The U.S. government owns the hibernation cave, and the maternity cave is on private property. The property owner has agreed to protect the bat "nursery" so that mothers and babies will be undisturbed.

Gray bats (below) are often tiny; some weigh as little as one-quarter ounce. Their colonies used to occupy several caves in Arkansas. Now, only one hibernation cave remains. The cave is home to about 250,000 of the little mammals. Gray bats have been listed as endangered since 1976, but their numbers are now increasing.

Indiana bats hibernate in clusters. Scientists have counted as many as 480 bats in 1 square foot of space. Fewer than three thousand Indiana bats remain in Arkansas.

The main reason the number of bats has fallen is that their caves have been disturbed or vandalized. The best way to protect them is to keep humans out of their habitats. One major hibernation cave in the Ozarks has been fenced off, and warning signs have been posted in four others. Environmentalists hope these efforts will help bats make a comeback in Arkansas.

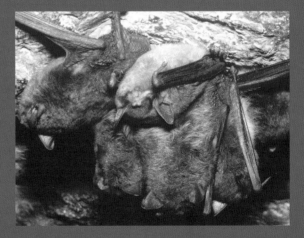

WILDLIFE IN DANGER

Plants and animals become endangered for many reasons. The most common reason is loss of habitat. These species are pushed out of their territory by other animals, by foreign species, or by people who develop the land to build homes or plant crops.

In Arkansas, twenty-one species of animals are listed as either threatened or endangered. These species include the American alligator, several kinds of fish, and a bird called the least tern. The endangered list includes six species of plants, such as the eastern prairie fringed orchid and the running buffalo clover. Some species, such as the Caddo Mountain salamander, are native only to Arkansas.

The American alligator is a threatened species. These individuals live in Hot Springs.

An endangered least tern protects its chicks.

PROTECTING THE ENVIRONMENT

Each September, Arkansas citizens take part in the Great Arkansas Cleanup. In 2006, fifty-five counties took part in the event. More than 20,000 volunteers picked up 4.4 million pounds of trash and cleaned up 4,077 miles of roadway and 1,048 miles of shoreline. They also closed forty-six illegal dumping sites. In 2005, state officials set up a toll-free hotline to encourage citizens to report littering. Arkansas is a leader in setting up a littering hotline. Only eight states have taken this step. "Our goal is to let Arkansans know this is a problem we take seriously and will pursue thoroughly through the enforcement of Arkansas's litter laws," said Ron Burks, chief of the Arkansas Highway Police.

Being a responsible citizen is a way of showing civic pride. The Great Arkansas Cleanup and the litter hotline show that Arkansans are proud of their Natural State.

Chapter Two

Back Then, in Arkansas

When Spanish explorer Hernando de Soto first saw Arkansas in 1541, he was looking for gold. There was no gold to be found, and de Soto died in Arkansas. Nearly 150 years later, the French explored the region. In 1682, René-Robert Cavelier, Sieur de La Salle, traveled down the Mississippi River to its mouth. He claimed the area for France and named it Louisiana in honor of King Louis XIV.

Henri de Tonti's account of Sieur de La Salle's expedition on the Mississippi River

France ceded the Louisiana territory to Spain in 1762. Spain ceded it back to France in 1800. Three years later, French leader Napoleon Bonaparte found himself in need of money to fight battles in Europe. He offered to sell the territory to the United States. In 1803, Napoleon and President Thomas Jefferson struck a deal for $11 million. The Louisiana Purchase doubled the size of the United States. Arkansas was only one part of the deal. In all, thirteen states were carved out of the vast territory that stretched all the way to the Rocky Mountains.

A strong sense of community has been a mainstay of Arkansas throughout its history. Here, friends enjoy a visit in 1905.

THE FIRST PEOPLE

Native Americans had been in Arkansas for thousands of years before Europeans arrived. Among the prehistoric peoples in the area were groups of Paleo-Indians formerly known as the Bluff Dwellers and the Mound Builders. The Bluff Dwellers lived in caves and rock shelters. They were nomads who wandered from place to place and ate from the bounty of the land. Men hunted game while women gathered edible plants. The Plum Bayou people, who were active beginning in the first century CE, built systematically arranged mounds surrounding open areas used for religious ceremonies and other gatherings.

At Toltec Mounds Archaeological State Park, visitors can see 39-foot-high mounds built by the Plum Bayou people.

The descendants of the Paleo-Indians were the Quapaw, Osage, and Caddo tribal groups. These groups were already well established in Arkansas when Europeans arrived. The Caddo lived in the southwestern part of the state, while the Osage spent part of the year living and hunting in the Ozarks. The Quapaw lived along the lower Arkansas River, near its junction with the Mississippi.

The Osage, Caddo, and Quapaw were skilled hunters. They also grew crops such as corn, beans, and squash. The Caddo lived in large, rounded thatched cottages, each of which housed many families. Although each family had its own area, families shared a central fire, which never was allowed to go out. Traditionally, men and women wore clothing made of deer and bison skins. These garments were decorated with beaded designs and fringes. They made their own pottery and decorated these objects with elaborate designs. When they came into contact with other native people and with European settlers, Arkansas's tribes traded the goods they made for objects brought by other people. The Quapaw built dwellings of earth and covered them with bark, while the Osage erected frameworks of saplings and covered them with woven mats.

A European visitor painted this portrait of Clermont, a chief of the Osage tribe.

The Chocktaw people lived in a village along the Arkansas River. They also owned a large strip of land in the western part of Arkansas. Although the government granted this land by treaty in 1820, the Chocktaw were forced to surrender it in 1825.

HOW COYOTE BROUGHT DEATH TO THE WORLD: A CADDO STORY

When the world was young, people lived forever. At first, this seemed a fine thing; but after a time, Earth ran out of room. New people could not be born because there was no place for them to live. The chiefs got together to decide what to do about this problem. One said that maybe everybody should have to die for a little while, so there wouldn't be so many people on Earth all at once.

This would never work, Coyote said. If all the people who died came back, there wouldn't be enough food to feed them all. The chiefs considered this, but they could not bring themselves to make anyone die forever. They built a house of grass, facing east, toward the rising sun. Here, they would call the spirit to enter the house and become alive again.

After the first man died, medicine men gathered in the grass house to call his spirit home. They called until a spirit-wind came and whirled around the grass house. Just as it reached the doorway, Coyote jumped up and closed the door. Finding no ways to get inside, the spirit-wind blew on by and soon was gone. The man who had died never returned. This is how Coyote brought death into the world and made it last forever.

The Cherokee people lived along the St. Francis River and the Arkansas River in the early 1800s. They traded skins and bear oil for European-made goods including iron kettles and guns. The Cherokee often came into conflict with the Osage tribe, which hunted regularly in northern Arkansas. Attacks between the two tribes were frequent, and Fort Smith was established so that soldiers could keep the two tribes apart.

White settlers gradually forced Arkansas's Native Americans off their tribal lands. Since 1835, when the Caddo were forced west of Arkansas's borders, there have been no tribal lands in the state.

BUILDING A TERRITORY

In 1686, Henri de Tonti, a member of La Salle's expedition, founded the first European settlement in what would become Arkansas. Only six people lived in this community, which later became known as Arkansas Post. For more than a hundred years, Arkansas was not widely settled by Europeans. As late as 1799, only 386 white people lived there.

In 1819, Arkansas became an official territory of the United States. Its boundaries were much the same as they are today, except the western border. Territorial Arkansas contained part of what is now Oklahoma.

That same year, an ambitious young printer named William E. Woodruff arrived at Arkansas Post. He had decided that the new territory needed a print shop and a newspaper of its own. On November 20, 1819, he put out the first issue of the *Arkansas Gazette*. When the territorial capital was transferred from Arkansas Post to the new town of Little Rock, Woodruff and the *Gazette* moved, too. This was the beginning of a genuine, homegrown Arkansas institution. The *Arkansas Gazette* lasted for 172 years. Its final issue went to press on October 18, 1991.

The *Gazette* shaped public opinion in many ways. For example, the territory had been called Akansea, Acansa, Akansas, and Arkansaw as well as Arkansas. Woodruff settled the matter with little fuss. He simply made sure that the *Gazette* used nothing but the word *Arkansas*, and before long it became the favored spelling.

Pronunciation was another issue. Was it AR-kan-SAW, in the French manner, or the state of KAN-sas with an *Ar* in front of it? Even politicians couldn't agree. At one point, the disagreement traveled all the way to the floor of the United States Senate, where one senator was always introduced as the senator from AR-kan-SAW and the other was called the senator from Ar-KAN-sas. The question wasn't answered officially until 1881, when the state legislature passed a resolution making *Arkansas* the official spelling and AR-kan-SAW the official pronunciation.

THE CHALLENGES OF STATEHOOD

Throughout the 1820s, more settlers moved to Arkansas. Families built homes. Townships planned courthouses and city halls. Gristmills and sawmills were scattered around the territory, and cotton farms were springing up throughout the South. By 1830, Arkansas had a population of 30,388. Admitted to the Union on June 15, 1836, it became the twenty-fifth state of the young republic.

Like most frontier societies, Arkansas's was rough, wild, and often lawless. Occasional scandals marked the early years of statehood. Shortly after becoming mayor of Little Rock, Samuel G. Trowbridge was arrested for burglary and counterfeiting money. "His Honor" turned out to be the mastermind behind a gang of criminals operating in the Little Rock area.

In this frontier society, even basically honest officials did things that would not be acceptable today. Beginning in the 1820s, three families dominated Arkansas politics: the Seviers, the Conways, and the Johnsons. They appointed relatives and close friends to important positions and handpicked their candidates for elected offices.

In 1836, William Woodruff resigned as editor of the *Gazette* in order to enter state government. A strong ally of the three powerful families, he became Arkansas's first state treasurer. In that position, Woodruff expected to receive a commission on land sold for back taxes and to have a free hand with his expense account. He received a rude awakening when the legislature denied his commission on the sale of land and cut almost half his expenses. Instead of making money from the treasurer's office,

William Woodruff founded Arkansas's first newspaper, the Arkansas Gazette.

the disappointed Woodruff ended up owing the state more than two thousand dollars for excess expenses. He chose not to run for another term.

Despite its political troubles, Arkansas grew. In 1840, the state had a population of more than 97,000 people. Nearly 20,000 of the state's people were enslaved Africans. By this time, the Northern states had outlawed slavery, but the Southern states had not. Arkansas's plantation culture was based on cotton farming, which required a plentiful supply of cheap labor. Northern abolitionists (activists who worked to end slavery) argued that slavery was inhumane, but Southern slaveholders refused to yield. This conflict, among others, triggered the bloodiest war in American history.

WE'RE COMING ARKANSAS

They say that a proposal was once introduced in the state legislature to change the name of Arkansas. No one knows whether this actually happened. Nevertheless, speeches purported to have been made in response to the proposal are part of Arkansas folklore. Compare the valley to a gorgeous sunrise, the discordant croak of the bullfrog to the melodious tones of a nightingale, the classic strains of Mozart to the bray of a Mexican mule . . . but never change the name of Arkansas.

com - ing, Ark - an - sas. We're com - ing, Ark - an - sas. Our

four-horse team will soon be seen on the road to Ark - an - sas.

The men keep hounds down there,
And hunting is all they care;
The women plough and hoe the corn,
While the men shoot turkey and deer. *Chorus*

The girls are strong down there,
Clean and healthy and gay,
They card and spin from morning till night
And dance from night till day. *Chorus*

They raise their 'baccer patch,
The women all smoke and chaw,
Eat hog, and hominy and poke for greens
Way down in Arkansas. *Chorus*

The roads are tough down there,
You must take um 'done or raw'
There's rocks and rills and stumps and hills
On the road to Arkansas. *Chorus*

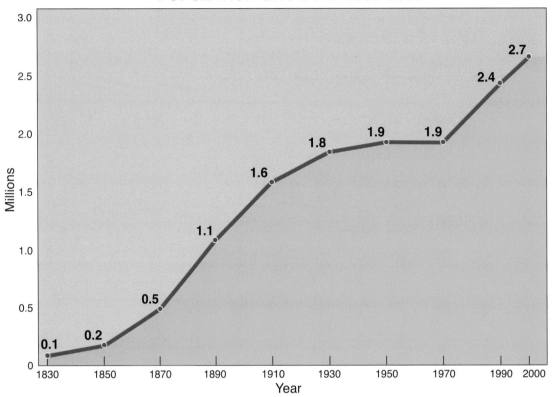

POPULATION GROWTH: 1830–2000

WAR AND RECONSTRUCTION

On April 12, 1861, Southern military forces attacked the U.S. Army garrison at Fort Sumter, South Carolina. The Civil War had begun.

Before this attack, South Carolina and six other states had seceded from the Union and had formed the Confederate States of America. In May, Arkansas followed their lead and became the ninth state to join the Confederacy.

Not everyone in Arkansas supported the Confederacy. In the mountains and high valleys of the northern part of the state, few people owned slaves, or cared to own them. Many of these people supported the Union, or at least they did not actively oppose it. Meanwhile, Arkansans with Confederate sympathies threw themselves into "the cause." For some people, this meant raising money for the war effort. For others, it meant the ultimate sacrifice. About 15,000 young Arkansans joined the Union army, while about 60,000 Arkansans fought for the Confederacy.

Although the Civil War battle of Pea Ridge took place in Arkansas, Union and Confederate troops were fighting for control of Missouri.

Arkansans still tell the story of David Owen Dodd. He was just seventeen years old when Union troops captured him near Little Rock. An innocent-looking notebook in his pocket contained a coded report on enemy troop strength in the area. Dodd was found guilty of spying and was sentenced to hang. Union general Frederick Steele offered a pardon in exchange for the names of others who helped gather the information. "I can die, but I cannot betray the trust of a friend," Dodd is said to have replied. He was hanged on schedule, and later he took his place in Arkansas legend. His grave is inscribed "Boy Martyr of the Confederacy."

In the end, heroism and dedication to the cause were not enough to win. By late 1863, Union forces occupied at least half of Arkansas. The Confederacy was defeated in 1865. For Arkansans returning from the war, a new struggle lay ahead. Veterans found their farms destroyed, their livestock and equipment gone, and their credit lost. Former slaves struggled to make a place for themselves in society. This was the beginning of Reconstruction. During this period, which lasted until 1877, the states of the former Confederacy were brought back into the Union gradually.

In Arkansas, as in the rest of the South, Reconstruction was a time of economic hardship, political corruption, and public uncertainty. Immediately after the war, the state legislature, which was composed largely of former Confederates, passed laws to restrict the freedom of former slaves. The Union army put a stop to this practice by placing Arkansas under military rule.

Home rule was not fully restored until Arkansas passed a new state constitution in 1874. Even then, African Americans did not have equal rights. The law was one thing; reality was another. Race remained a defining issue for Arkansas and the rest of the Old South.

CELEBRATING HISTORY

Festivals with historic themes are popular in Arkansas. Every October, the town of Evening Shade holds the Annual Founder's Day and Pioneer Rendezvous, when residents transform the modern town into a frontier settlement of 1847. Local people dress in period costume and encourage visitors to do the same. People come to town on horseback or in wagons to listen to old-time, foot-stomping music and to sample homemade sweets from an enormous dessert table.

The Annual Civil War Weekend at Lake Chicot State Park is living history at its best. The event features complete Confederate and Union army camps, demonstrations of Civil War artillery and firearms, and music and dancing from the period. The climax of the three-day event is a reenactment of the Engagement at Ditch Bayou.

A generation after the Civil War ended slavery, a series of new laws established racial segregation, or separation, in the South. These Jim Crow laws, named after a minstrel show character, divided the South into two distinct groups: one white, the other black. Hotels, cafés, theaters, public bathrooms, and even water fountains were segregated. An African American who drank at a "whites only" fountain or entered a "whites only" restroom could be arrested.

Daisy Bates (left), state president of the NAACP, pickets Little Rock department stores because they offer "dual service"—good for whites, bad for blacks. The date is April 15, 1960, during the time of Jim Crow laws.

THE TWENTIETH CENTURY

By 1900, Arkansas had a population of 1.3 million, and the majority of its workers was employed in agriculture. Industrialization and modernization lagged behind much of the country until 1921, when oil production began on a major scale. Deposits were found near the town of El Dorado in the southern part of the state. Suddenly, office buildings, hotels, schools, and electric lines sprang up all over the state. Roads that had been dirt trails became paved highways.

The Great Flood and Other Disasters

This modernization was stopped in its tracks in 1927, when the greatest flood known in American history hit Arkansas and its neighbors. That spring, the rains never seemed to end. It rained ten times the yearly average. On April 15, 1927, the Mississippi River's levees failed, and water flooded the entire region. The Mississippi River and its tributaries filled to their banks and then spread out over the land. The Mississippi itself covered much of Arkansas as well as Missouri, Mississippi, Texas, Louisiana, and Illinois. One writer called it "the greatest flood since Noah's." It left thousands of people homeless, hundreds dead, and whole towns utterly destroyed. Farmland was useless because it was so waterlogged.

Nature was not through with Arkansas. Three years after the flood, there was a drought. Crops withered in the fields, and topsoil blew away in great swirls of wind.

Waters from the Great Flood force people to use boats to travel through the town of Lake Village.

As if Arkansas had not suffered enough, the stock market crashed in 1929. The resulting Great Depression threw the whole country into economic chaos. Arkansas suffered along with the rest of the nation. Farmers lost their land, families lost their homes, and thousands of hardworking people lost their jobs.

An Arkansas family camps by the road in Imperial County, California, after leaving their home during the Depression in May 1937.

Wartime

In time, both the drought and the Depression ended, but the economy didn't get a boost until the United States entered World War II in 1941. For many young Arkansans, the war offered a chance both to serve their country and to enjoy guaranteed food, a roof (or a tent) over their heads, and income. Although nearly 200,000 Arkansans served in the war, the rejection rate of 43 percent reflected the poor health and education of the young people of the state. Other rural Arkansans sought better-paying defense industry jobs. There were military-supply plants in Camden, Jacksonville, Hope, and Pine Bluff. These plants also introduced many Arkansan women to paid work. Of the 13,000 workers at the plant in Jacksonville, three-quarters were women.

At the same time, military bases in the state became the temporary homes of 23,000 German and Italian prisoners of war. Arkansas also housed many Japanese Americans who were taken from their homes on the West Coast because they were considered to be loyalty risks. Although the prisoners of war were sent home after the conflict ended, several returned to Arkansas as civilians and settled in the state permanently.

Black Arkansans serving in World War II continued to be segregated from white soldiers, both on army bases in Arkansas and on the battlefields of Europe. In 1948, President Harry Truman signed an order that ended segregation in the

The first of 4,500 Japanese-American prisoners are moved from the Santa Anita Assembly Center in California to the new Rohwer Relocation Camp in Desha County in September 1942.

U.S. armed forces. It would take extraordinary bravery and a hard-fought civil rights movement in the late 1950s and 1960s, however, to change laws that denied African Americans basic rights such as voting and a quality education.

THE LITTLE ROCK NINE

On September 25, 1957, nine African-American students walked to the front door of Central High School in Little Rock. They were there to start school, but they were also there to integrate a school that had educated only white students. They had the law on their side. In 1954, the Supreme Court of the United States had outlawed segregation in schools. In Arkansas, however, schools faced Governor Orval Faubus, who was determined to resist integration ordered by the federal government. The nine students—Ernest Green, Melba Patillo, Minnijean Brown, Thelma Mothershed, Gloria Ray, Terrance Roberts, Carlotta Walls, Jefferson Thomas, and Elizabeth Eckford—were about to make civil rights history.

Of these nine, Elizabeth Eckford is perhaps best remembered. At the time she was fifteen years old, bright, and eager for a good education. On September 4, 1957, she walked alone through the screaming mob that stood between her and the front door of the school. When she tried to enter, Arkansas National Guardsmen barred the way. Press photographer Will Counts captured Elizabeth's bravery on film. While Elizabeth faced the mob, the other eight students were gathering a few blocks away. The Arkansas National Association for the Advancement of Colored People had arranged for the teenagers to go to school as a group. Somehow, Elizabeth had never gotten the word. The eight other students also tried to enter the school that day, with the same result. President Dwight D. Eisenhower sent U.S. Army troops to protect the students and to keep the peace. Three weeks later, the

National Guardsmen bar Elizabeth Eckford (holding notebook) from Central High School under orders from Governor Orval Faubus on September 4, 1957.

Little Rock Nine, as the students came to be called, finally walked through the schoolhouse door.

Despite the army escort, it was a frightening day for the nine young people. "All I could hear was my own heartbeat and the sound of boots clicking on stone," recalled Melba Patillo Beals. For many white onlookers, who grew up accepting racism as a normal part of life, September 25 was a day of horror. According to reporter Relman Morin, as the nine mounted the steps, white women in the crowd were crying to police officers, "They are in our school, Oh God, are you going to stand there and let them stay in school?"

In 1997, forty years later, the Little Rock Nine returned to Central High School and were met by applause and flashing cameras. Former president Bill Clinton and former Arkansas governor Mike Huckabee made speeches praising the students' courage. Former president Clinton, himself an Arkansan, talked about that dark day: "We saw not one nation under God, indivisible, with liberty and justice for all, but two Americas, divided and unequal. What happened here changed the course of our country."

On August 30, 2005, the Little Rock Nine were honored in their hometown when a magnificent bronze sculpture depicting the nine teens was placed on the grounds of the Arkansas State Capitol in Little Rock. All nine attended the ceremony and took part in the unveiling of the monument, entitled *Testament*. Tears flowed freely from the former students and onlookers alike as they looked at the monument.

In 2007, an international symposium commemorating the fiftieth anniversary of Central High School's integration was held at the University of Arkansas. Arkansas high school students competed for scholarships in an essay and art contest. The Little Rock Nine attended a ceremony held on the lawn of Central High School. Also in 2007, the U.S. Mint introduced a silver dollar coin to commemorate the Little Rock Nine. One side depicts the students being escorted by a soldier, with the phrase " Desegregation in Education." The other side shows Central High School in 1957.

A monument to the Little Rock Nine stands outside the capitol.

ARKANSAS TODAY AND TOMORROW

In spite of the achievement of the Little Rock Nine, true racial integration—and social progress—happened slowly in Arkansas. While the civil rights movement of the 1960s was gaining strength in parts of the United States, Arkansas remained resistant to integration. When a sit-in movement began in an attempt to integrate facilities, protesters were jailed and fined for daring to challenge the idea that white and black people should have equal rights and access. As African Americans joined organizations such as the Student Nonviolent Coordinating Committee, known nationally as SNCC, white opposition became stronger.

In 1965, Arkansas legislators made it easier for African Americans to vote by abolishing the poll tax and passing the Voting Rights Act of 1965. One of the key figures in this achievement was Winthrop Rockefeller, the first Republican governor in Arkansas since 1874.

After the assassination of Dr. Martin Luther King Jr. in 1968, anger in Arkansas led to violent clashes between blacks and whites. By the 1970s, African Americans were gaining ground in Arkansas's government, and the Arkansas Senate saw the election of its first black member, Dr. Jerry Jewell. An impressive 94 percent of eligible African-American Arkansans were registered to vote in 1976.

Genuine integration continued to elude Arkansas. Whites fled the Mississippi Delta and the cities for all-white suburbs. This resulted in newly segregated school systems. It became impossible to integrate school systems when the white students simply moved away.

In matters of local government, Arkansas has made great changes. Following the election of Winthrop Rockefeller, the state adopted a freedom of information act and its first minimum-wage act. In 1976, William Clinton was elected attorney general and began a vigorous program of social

CLINTON PRESIDENTIAL LIBRARY

On November 18, 2004, the William J. Clinton Presidential Library officially opened on the banks of the Arkansas River in Little Rock. The library has almost 80 million documents, 1.85 million photographs, and a museum with about 75,000 artifacts. It is also home to the Clinton School of Public Service. Former president Clinton describes the building itself as "the symbol of a bridge to the twenty-first century" because of the way it juts out over the Arkansas River. A 110-foot timeline takes visitors through the events that marked the Clinton White House years from 1993 to 2000. The library can be reached by trolley from downtown Little Rock.

improvements. As governor, Clinton brought a politically liberal point of view to the state.

The changing role of the National Guard helps illustrate the changes in Arkansas during the fifty years since the Little Rock Nine struggled to enter Central High School. Today, these "citizen soldiers" are often found on the front lines of emergencies rather than at the sites of racial conflict. After Hurricane Katrina hit the Southeast on August 29, 2005, National Guard troops were called in to help with the rescue effort. An Arkansas National Guardsman said, "We were an air medivac unit, pulling people off rooftops in Katrina."

Since the attack on New York City's World Trade Center on September 11, 2001, however, the National Guard has become more of a military fighting unit than a group of soldiers dedicated to helping Americans at home. The 39th Infantry Brigade Combat Team, based in Little Rock, was deployed to serve in Afghanistan and Iraq. In spite of losses in these wars, young Arkansans continue to sign up for the National Guard. One young recruiter said, "Southern states are the most represented in the [National] Guard. There's an attitude here of patriotism."

Even well into the twenty-first century, Arkansas has not lost touch with its past. The state's rich folk cultures have become sources of pride. Tourists come from all over the nation and the world to experience these traditions and to enjoy the state's natural beauty. For their part, many Arkansans have decided that living slightly off the beaten track suits them just fine.

Arkansas National Guardsmen from the 39th Infantry Brigade prepare for deployment to Iraq in February 2004.

Chapter Three

A Proud People

Tradition is important in Arkansas. People feel connected to the land, to one another, and to the values they consider timeless. The result is a society whose people are comfortable with themselves and not especially concerned with being trendy. In a changing world, many people enjoy that kind of stability.

"No matter how far away you go, or how famous you get, there's always Arkansas," said one longtime resident. "You can come back home, and it won't be all that different from when you left."

A SNAPSHOT

Arkansas's population has changed dramatically in the last decade. Most of the state's citizens are white descendants from early waves of immigrants from Ireland, Scotland, Germany, and England. Recently, however, Arkansas has experienced a surge in its Latino (Hispanic) and Asian populations. Latinos are moving into the state at a faster rate than anywhere else in the nation, although their overall numbers are still relatively small. With a surge of new and different people, the culture of Arkansas is changing significantly.

As Arkansas's people and culture change, traditions and friendships remain strong.

POPULATION DENSITY

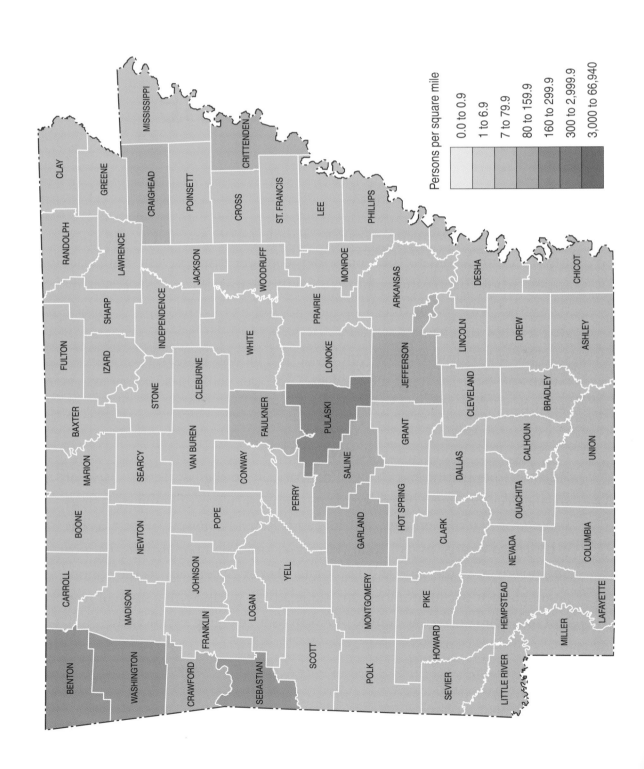

Persons per square mile

0.0 to 0.9
1 to 6.9
7 to 79.9
80 to 159.9
160 to 299.9
300 to 2,999.9
3,000 to 66,940

According to 2005 U.S. Census Bureau estimates, Arkansas's population is 16 percent African American. Blacks have played a major role in shaping the state's culture throughout its history. Today's African-American Arkansans face some alarming trends, however. According to the U.S. Census Bureau's 2000 figures, more than 30 percent of black Arkansans live in poverty. African Americans also suffer higher rates of death—especially infant death—than either the white or the Latino populations in the state.

Arkansas's residents and organizations have been working hard to change these statistics and to create better lives for African-American citizens.

The population of Arkansas is about 16 percent African American. Here, a boy plays with bubbles at Riverfest in Little Rock.

The Arkansas Baptist College School of Business and Applied Science is devoted to the higher education of black students. It emphasizes critical thinking, research, and leadership along with high ethical standards. Arkansas was the birthplace of John Johnson, publisher of *Jet* and *Ebony* magazines. Johnson was inducted into the Arkansas Business Hall of Fame in 2001 and was honored by the formation of the John H. Johnson Delta Cultural and Entrepreneurial Center in Arkansas City, the town of his birth.

RELIGION

The presence of Christianity and its role in the lives of Arkansans is evident throughout the state. Arkansans express their belief in Christianity quite differently in different regions of the state. Cultural differences are strongly expressed through traditions that are passed down from generation to generation. These traditions and beliefs help some people direct their lives in the face of very little material wealth.

In a recent survey of Arkansans, 86 percent identified themselves as Christians. Most of them were part of a Protestant denomination, while 7 percent said they were Catholics. With the increasing number of Latino residents in the state, the percentage of Catholics is rising rapidly.

The Hmong—an ethnic group from southern China, Vietnam, Thailand, and Laos—bring their own traditional religious beliefs to Arkansas. Many Hmong believe that the divine spirit can be found in all living things. They are deeply spiritual and maintain close connections with their ancestors. Once Hmong people settle in Arkansas, they often convert to Christianity.

An estimated three thousand Jewish people live in Arkansas today. The state's Jewish community is based in Little Rock. With the growth of business in the Bentonville area, a new group of Jews has emerged.

This church in Stuttgart is one of many Christian houses of worship in the state.

MUSEUMS AND THE ARTS

Arkansas boasts many new art museums and other cultural attractions in addition to the traditional cultures that have always been a hallmark of the state. Little Rock leads the way with its Arkansas Arts Center, while Russellville's Arkansas River Valley Arts Center is a center of visual and performing arts. In Pine Bluff, the Arts and Science Center for Southeast Arkansas draws visitors from throughout the state and beyond. Other cultural centers are located in Hot Springs, Fayetteville, and Stuttgart.

Crystal Bridges is a brand-new, world-class museum of art in Bentonville. The museum, dedicated to showcasing American art, was founded by Alice Walton and is backed by the huge Wal-Mart fortune. The enormous museum complex rivals first-class museums around the world and features important examples of American painting, including works by Gilbert Stuart and Winslow Homer. In addition to honoring these well-known artists, the museum shows regional and Native-American art. Crystal Bridges is housed in a building designed by Israel-born architect Moshe Safdie.

OZARKS CULTURE

In the knobs and hollers of the Ozarks, old mountain ways are still alive. Some people practice folk crafts such as whittling, pottery making, and quilting. They go hunting and berrying in the woods, and they use herbs to treat common illnesses. They dance to the music of the fiddle, the banjo, and the mountain dulcimer, a stringed instrument that is plucked like a banjo and produces a vibrating, metallic sound. Musicians sing with a high-pitched sound called a high lonesome wail. Cooks make traditional foods that their families enjoyed many generations ago.

In Mountain View, a small town in north-central Arkansas, the music of the Ozarks comes to life most Saturday nights. Fiddlers from all over the region come to town and set up their chairs around the Mountain View Courthouse. The music varies from group to group, but it all has a bluegrass or hill sound. Locals come by regularly to listen and sometimes to take part in the entertainment.

Traditional Ozark cooking includes beans, corn bread, and greens. Collard and turnip greens are the most popular types of greens. Greens are often seasoned with salt and fatback (salt pork) and then simmered until they soften. "If your greens still look pretty, it's for sure and certain they haven't boiled long enough," said one experienced cook.

A worker makes dulcimers for traditional folk music in Mountain View.

Other staples of Ozark cooking are pork, corn, and sorghum molasses, which is made from sorghum cane instead of sugar cane (sorghum is a type of tropical grass). Early settlers used molasses in place of sugar, which was expensive and hard to get. Today's Arkansan cooks use molasses in recipes that need its special flavor.

ARKANSAS CORN BREAD

Nothing says Arkansas better than a pan of fresh corn bread. This recipe is quick and easy.

1 cup cornmeal
1 cup unbleached flour
1/4 cup sugar
1 tablespoon baking powder

1 teaspoon salt
1/3 cup shortening
1 egg
1 cup milk

What to do:

1. Preheat the oven to 400 °F.
2. Measure cornmeal, flour, sugar, baking powder, and salt into a large bowl and mix them together.
3. In another bowl, mix shortening, egg, and milk.
4. Stir the shortening mixture into the dry ingredients. Mix just enough to blend the ingredients into a thick batter.
5. Rub an 8-inch square baking pan with butter.
6. Pour the batter into the pan.
7. Get an adult to help with the baking. Your corn bread should bake for 25 minutes.
8. After it is done baking, cut the corn bread into squares. For a traditional Arkansas-style breakfast, butter a piece of hot corn bread and top it with molasses.

If Arkansas had an official state dish, however, it would probably be barbecue—meat smoked at a low temperature for a long period of time. Arkansans have endless debates about the best barbecue restaurant, the best cooking method, and the best sauce. Barbecue is popular throughout the Southern states. The Arkansas version is unique for its focus on chicken (due to the state's strong poultry industry), and its sauces tend to be spicier than those of neighboring states.

These soul food restaurant owners are proud of their chicken barbecue.

SPIRIT OF THE FRONTIER

Near its border with Oklahoma and Texas, Arkansas feels like the Old West. In these areas, many people work as cattle ranchers and lumberjacks. Western dress is common, rodeos are a big draw, and a thick steak is some of the best eating around. Musicians are more likely to play electric guitars than mountain dulcimers. When they sing, a country-western twang replaces the high lonesome wail of the mountains.

In the old days, western Arkansas was a true frontier. It had everything—outlaws, saloon brawls, and an occasional shootout in the streets of a dusty cow town. It even had a genuine "hangin' judge." Citizens of Fort Smith recall Judge Isaac Parker, who sentenced eighty-eight criminals to hang during his twenty-one years on the bench.

A cowgirl at a dude ranch shows the Western flair of her state.

DELTA LIFE

On the Mississippi Delta, life moves with the rhythms of the river, and Southern hospitality still matters. The people here are mainly farmers, working some of the richest soil in the country. Their work is seasonal, often backbreaking, and usually low paid.

The delta is home to many African Americans. Some still farm the land that their enslaved ancestors worked. As black people in a white-dominated society, African Americans still face many challenges. Racial segregation is no longer legal in Arkansas, but in practice it still exists in some places. Blacks and whites often live in separate neighborhoods, for example. White people control most local governments, police departments, and social-service agencies.

Arkansas's African-American culture has a strong base in religion. In black communities up and down the delta, Sunday is a day for "preaching, praying, and praising," as one minister put it. Congregations that don't have a church of their own meet in storefronts or in people's homes. If they don't have a preacher, a member of the congregation will offer up a few words. If they don't have someone who can play the piano, the congregation sings unaccompanied.

Outside of church, the Mississippi Delta's traditional music is the blues, with its strong beat and moody lyrics. The picturesque river town of Helena is noted for its blues clubs. Helena is also the home of the *King Biscuit Time* radio program, which has aired since November 1941. A genuine Arkansas institution, the program still broadcasts the blues Monday through Friday to listeners throughout the region. The 2000 film *O Brother, Where Art Thou?* features a delta deejay who opens his program by saying, "Pass the biscuits." This is the opening phrase of *King Biscuit Time*'s host, Sunshine Sonny Paine.

NEWCOMERS

Arkansas is becoming an increasingly multicultural society. In recent years, the state has attracted immigrants from Asia and Latin America. These newcomers practice unique traditions, speak many different languages, and practice religions that are still fairly new to the state.

In the mid-1970s, Hmong, Vietnamese, and other Southeast Asian people fled war-torn homelands for a new life in the United States. Some settled in the Mississippi Delta and found work in rice fields much like those they left behind in Asia. Others went to the cities. Most Southeast Asian newcomers practice the religion of Buddhism.

Customers enjoy Asian cuisine at a Japanese restaurant in Little Rock.

In the 1990s, thousands of Latinos moved to Arkansas from Central and South America in search of economic opportunity. Their native tongue is Spanish, and for the most part their religion is Catholicism. The flourishing poultry industry drew many Latinos to the northwest corner of the state, next to Oklahoma and Missouri. According to 2005 estimates, Latinos make up about 5 percent of Arkansas's population. They are growing at a faster rate than any other ethnic group. For example, the Latino population in Benton County nearly doubled from 12,000 to 24,000 in 2005.

The Hispanic population of Arkansas is growing rapidly.

Businesses and local governments are working hard to help Latinos become part of the community. In Arkansas City, a small town on the border with Tennessee, a grocery store called Country Mart introduced many Latino foods into its stock. This was in response to an influx of Mexican immigrants who were working at a new local packing plant. Home Town Rental, an appliance-rental store, hired bilingual employees who can translate for Latino customers.

In the town of Rogers, not far from Wal-Mart's headquarters, the Latino population increased to 20 percent between 1990 and 2000.

ETHNIC ARKANSAS

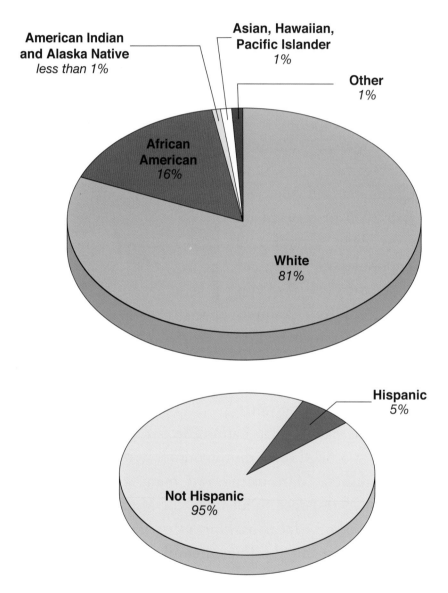

**American Indian
and Alaska Native**
less than 1%

**Asian, Hawaiian,
Pacific Islander**
1%

Other
1%

**African
American**
16%

White
81%

Hispanic
5%

Not Hispanic
95%

*Note: A person of Cuban, Mexican, Puerto Rican, South or Central American,
or other Spanish culture or origin, regardless of race, is defined as Hispanic.*

Like many other towns in Arkansas, Rogers did not have the resources to handle this dramatic increase in non-English-speaking residents. The town's officials traveled around the country in search of people in other small towns that had experienced a similar shift in population. The transition is in its early stages. Arkansas is one of many states adapting to recent waves of immigration that are changing the face of the United States.

LEGENDARY ARKANSAS

Arkansas folklore is a rich tradition created by natural storytellers. The tall tale, also called a windy, is a specialty of the state. A good windy is based on exaggeration—the hero so strong he could whip his weight in wildcats, the weather so hot it made corn pop in the fields, or the cabin so small you had to step outside to change your mind.

Sometimes the windy is a joke, and sometimes it's a game. A joke uses wild exaggeration to get a laugh. A game is more complicated—the teller spins a lengthy tale to see how far he or she can go before the listener realizes what's happening.

A popular relative of the windy is the "eyewitness" account of some outlandish creature. The catywhompus is an Ozark classic. It is a shaggy animal with two long legs on one side of its body and two short legs on the other. The catywhompus is built for racing around mountains. It can only go in one direction because the longer legs must always be on the "down" side. On the flats, the poor thing can't budge.

Arkansas folklore is full of monstrous creatures, not all of them as humorous as the catywhompus. For example, many people believed in the White River monster. Off and on for more than a hundred years, people have reported seeing a monster in the river. The monster was as big as a boxcar, with a smooth gray hide and a knack for appearing just often enough to keep its legend alive. Like the abominable snowman, the White River monster never could be captured or photographed. No one could say where it lived or why it stayed in the river. It was a mystery, and Arkansans love a mystery—particularly if it has a hint of the monstrous.

In 1973, Arkansas's state legislature decided to honor the legend by creating the White River Monster Refuge. Lawmakers carefully described the borders of this preserve and made a formal resolution that "no monster may be molested, killed or trampled" in the sanctuary.

THE GHOST TRAIN OF BOONE COUNTY

Up Boone County way, folks know a ghost when they see one—even if the ghost happens to be a train. You see, some years back, the Missouri and North Arkansas Railroad ran through there. Right from the start, that ole' M&NA gave passengers and station agents fits.

Doggone thing was never on time. It passed up places it was supposed to stop, and stopped at places it was supposed to pass. When it finally got where it was going, all the passengers would be in a tizzy and half the baggage would be lost.

Folks took to calling the M&NA the old May-Never-Arrive. Long after the railroad shut down, hoboes camping under the trestle would see a caboose racing down the tracks in the moonlight. Dern thing never made a sound. It just rolled on for a spell, then up and disappeared.

Those hoboes thought they'd seen some devilish goings-on, but the local folks told 'em not to worry. It was just the ghost of the old May-Never-Arrive, bein' late to its own funeral.

FACING THE FUTURE

For most of its history, Arkansas has seemed like a cultural time capsule, populated by hardy, God-fearing folk who were generally happy with their lot in life. When the Little Rock Nine forced Arkansans to face their own racism, new issues appeared. Arkansans grappled with those issues as best they could. For many, change was both slow and painful.

The creation of a broader and more tolerant society is an ongoing process. Many Arkansans are opening themselves to other cultures while protecting—and sharing—their own cherished values. In the future, when today's schoolchildren look back, they will see just how much their state has changed.

The students at Portland Elementary School illustrate increased integration in the cultural backgrounds of Arkansas's people.

Chapter Four

Governing Arkansas

In Arkansas, even the highest levels of government and industry function with a kind of down-home coziness. When former president Bill Clinton was governor of Arkansas, he spoke about this closeness: "In my state, when people lose their jobs, there's a good chance I'll know them by their names. When a factory closes, I know the people who ran it. When the businesses go bankrupt, I know them."

In the information age, Arkansas leaders are blending old-fashioned neighborliness with the latest in high-tech communications. Their goal is to make government more responsive to the people.

INSIDE GOVERNMENT

Arkansas's state government follows the federal government's model. It has three independent but interrelated branches: executive, legislative, and judicial.

Executive Branch

The governor is the chief executive officer of the state. He or she serves a four-year term, and there is a two-term limit. The governor draws up the

Government officials do the business of the state at the capitol in Little Rock.

state's budget, appoints members of various departments and commissions, and proposes laws and economic programs to the legislature.

Other positions in the executive branch include lieutenant governor, secretary of state, treasurer, auditor, land commissioner, and attorney general. People in these positions help the governor carry out the many tasks related to managing a state.

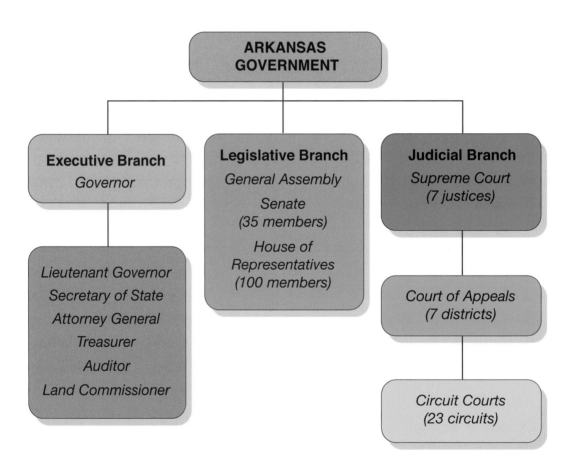

Most of Arkansas's governors have belonged to the Democratic Party. In the history of the state, only seven Republicans have occupied the governor's office. Four of them served during the period of Reconstruction that followed the Civil War. Not until 1967 would another Republican occupy the statehouse. Winthrop Rockefeller seemed an unlikely choice for the job. He was not only a Republican but also a northerner and a member of one of the richest families in the United States. He went to Arkansas because he had investments in the state, and he stayed because he liked the pace of life.

Winthrop's grandfather was the legendary John D. Rockefeller, one of the founders of the Standard Oil Company. Winthrop's brother Nelson was governor of New York and later would become vice president of the United States under Gerald Ford. Winthrop Rockefeller served two terms as governor of Arkansas. After losing his bid for a third term in 1970, he moved to Palm Springs, California.

The Rockefeller family's association with Arkansas did not end with Winthrop's death. His son, Winthrop Paul Rockefeller, became lieutenant governor in 1996 and served until his death on July 16, 2006.

Arkansas governor Winthrop Rockefeller poses in 1968.

Legislative Branch

Arkansas's state legislature, the Arkansas General Assembly, is made up of a senate with thirty-five members and a house of representatives with one hundred members. State senators serve four-year terms, while representatives serve two-year terms.

The legislature makes the laws for the state. Members of committees such as education, public health, and economic development study proposed laws in their areas. For example, the education committee might debate standards for teacher certification, while the economic development committee might propose laws to help people start new businesses. When a committee sends a bill (proposed law) to the legislature, it must pass both the house and the senate before it is sent to the governor to be signed into law.

Service in Arkansas's legislature is part-time. Most senators and representatives have full-time jobs outside of government service. For example, in 2007, the Arkansas Senate included the director of a nursing home, the owner of a recycling company, a bank president, a rancher, two farmers, an engineer, a pastor, the director of a funeral home, and a building contractor. Holding down these jobs while also serving in local government gives the legislators a genuine connection with the people they represent.

In 2005, the Arkansas General Assembly passed Act 907, which authorizes the state police to seek training on immigration enforcement from federal immigration officials. This gives state troopers the right to stop people they suspect of violating immigration laws. This is a controversial law because people feel differently about the presence—and rights—of illegal immigrants in the state.

Judicial Branch

The Arkansas Supreme Court is the state's highest court. The supreme court has a chief justice and six associate justices, who are elected for eight-year terms. Until 1978, the supreme court was the only appellate court in the state. Someone who wanted to challenge a ruling of a lower court had nowhere else to go.

When the supreme court's workload became too heavy, the state created a six-judge court of appeals. Now, most appeals go to the court of appeals. In many cases, the appeal ends there. If the person filing the appeal is still not satisfied, he or she may request a hearing before the state supreme court. Cases that involve a possible death penalty or that require an interpretation of the state constitution go directly to the supreme court. These two courts have devel-

A local courthouse in Pine Bluff

oped a fast-track system for hearing cases. In many states, an appeal can take months. In Arkansas, the goal is to produce a judicial decision within two weeks of the filing of an appeal.

Arkansas's main trial courts are circuit, or district, courts. More than one hundred judges, who are elected to four-year terms, preside over these courts. Chancery courts handle domestic cases and other civil matters. There are also county courts and municipal (city) courts to manage cases at the local level.

ARKANSAS QUARTER

The Arkansas quarter, one of a series of quarters honoring the fifty United States, was issued by the U.S. Mint in October 2003. Arkansas's was the twenty-fifth quarter to be minted. (The order of the coins' release reflected the order in which the states were admitted into the Union.) Each state chose the symbols used on its quarter. The Arkansas quarter pays tribute to the state's natural resources in honor of its nickname, the Natural State. A diamond, stalks of rice, and a mallard are arranged around a lake and a forest. Nearly 458 million Arkansas quarters were issued.

COUNTY GOVERNMENT

Arkansas has a large number of counties for a state with such a small population. Each of its seventy-five counties is run by a county seat and associated officials. Each county can enact laws that are in effect only in that county. For example, forty-two of Arkansas's seventy-five counties are considered "dry," meaning it is illegal to sell or to drink alcoholic beverages. Only ten of those counties are considered totally dry, however. The remaining counties allow alcohol to be served in a private setting, such as a country club.

EDUCATION AND HUMAN SERVICES

Arkansas has a solid system of schools and human services. Although the budget for services is limited, officials generally use the available money well. For example, the Arkansas Division of Children and Family Services uses the Internet to seek adoptive families for hard-to-place children.

ARKANSAS BY COUNTY

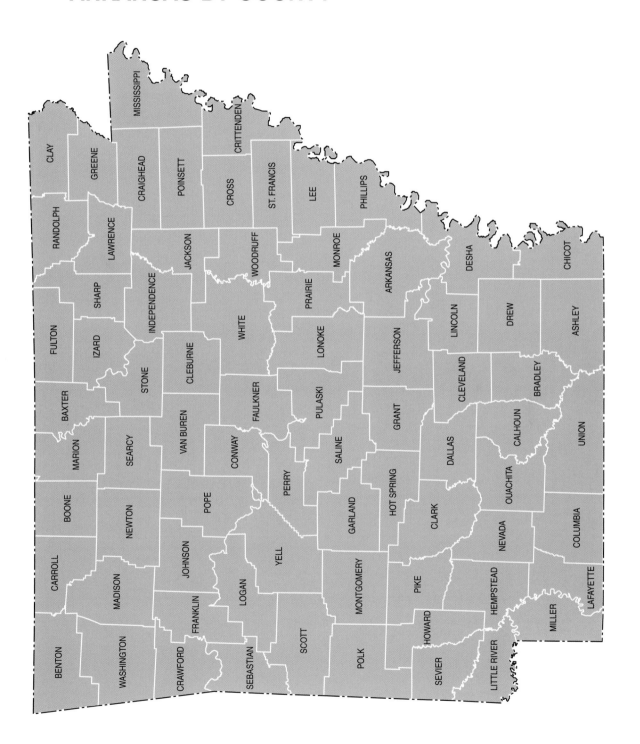

Arkansas's government is devoting valuable resources to its schools. Pictured here is a school in Little Rock.

Its Web site includes a photo and a biography of each child and explains his or her situation and needs.

Arkansas's public school system has a thriving system of magnet schools. These schools specialize in certain subjects and draw students interested in those subjects from across district lines. Crystal Hill Elementary Magnet School in North Little Rock specializes in communications. Students at Crystal Hill learn about computers and the Internet, produce their own video projects, and learn how to use other communications technologies. They also study more traditional subjects related to communications, such as photography, journalism, drama, and public speaking.

Horace Mann Arts and Science Magnet Middle School is in Little Rock's east end. It became an arts and sciences school in 1987. At Horace Mann, art students can study visual arts, drama, dance, and music, while science students get to work in an experimental laboratory. The school draws talented students from across the city. "There are more opportunities to do stuff here. It's more hands-on than other schools," said student Andrea Anderson. "I came here because I wanted to be in band," said Fred McKindra. "The band director is one of the best in Arkansas."

Chapter Five

Arkansas at Work

Arkansas now employs more people in service industries than in any other industry. Just over one-third of the state's workforce is employed in various kinds of services. Many of these jobs are in the tourism industry, which brought in $4.25 billion in 2004. Two areas of Arkansas have enjoyed an upswing in tourism: the Ozarks and the Ouachita Mountain region. Services account for more than half of Arkansas's income. This is an enormous change in a state that has relied heavily on agriculture and manufacturing for much of its history.

According to U.S. Census Bureau statistics on personal income, Arkansas ranks toward the bottom of the fifty states. In 2005, Arkansas scored higher than just two other states, Mississippi and Louisiana. The state's business and government leaders are working hard to turn the economy around and to establish a place for Arkansas in the global market.

EMPLOYMENT OPPORTUNITIES

Many of Arkansas's educated, skilled workers find employment in the northwest and center of the state. The northwest is home to the University of

Arkansas is the largest producer of rice in the United States.

Arkansas in Fayetteville, as well as Wal-Mart, the biggest retail business in the world, in nearby Bentonville. The center of the state includes the capital city, Little Rock, which has experienced an employment boom in the twenty-first century.

The leaders of Arkansas's growing industries are seeking out workers with high levels of education and advanced degrees in emerging fields. Wireless communications grew the most in 2006, with an increase of nearly two thousand jobs. The greatest loss of jobs was in the textile furnishings mills. Even though the entire nation has experienced a loss of jobs in this industry, the loss in Arkansas was dramatic. Nearly half the state's textile-mill jobs disappeared in 2006. Like most manufacturing jobs that have disappeared in the United States, these jobs are now done in China.

ARKANSAS WORKFORCE

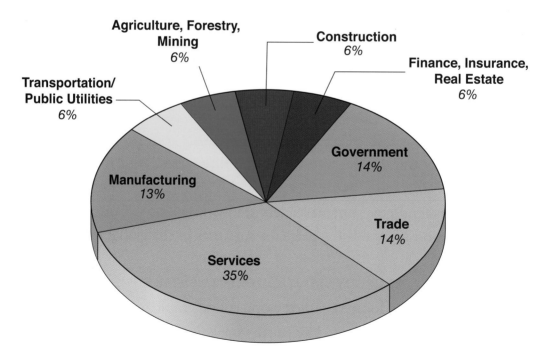

BIGGEST RETAILER IN THE WORLD

A big change in Arkansas's economy came from just one company: Wal-Mart. The largest retailer in the world was started by Sam Walton in a small store in Bentonville. When Walton opened his first Wal-Mart store in 1962, he had only one goal: to sell products at the cheapest price possible. Today, Wal-Mart brings in more money than every company except Exxon-Mobil. Wal-Mart employs 1.8 million people worldwide and has made the Walton family the richest family in the United States. The company's headquarters are still in Bentonville, in the northwest part of the state. Wal-Mart has attracted many other businesses to that corner of Arkansas. Although most of the new companies do not manufacture products in Arkansas, they have opened offices there in order to do business with Wal-Mart.

Although Wal-Mart's 2006 income topped $315 billion, the company is known for paying its employees poorly. The company keeps its labor costs as low as possible. As a result, nearly half the children of Wal-Mart's employees either have no health insurance or are eligible for Medicaid, the U.S. government program for people who are too poor to afford health care.

Although Arkansas had about 22,000 more workers in mid-2006 than in the year before, the poorest areas did not benefit from this growth. The greatest amounts of new jobs were in Benton County, home to Wal-Mart, and Pulaski County, home to Little Rock.

On May 17, 2007, England OilField Services announced that it would build a manufacturing facility in England, Arkansas. It promised to offer 175 new, well-paying jobs. Governor Mike Beebe announced a community development grant of more than $1.3 million to help fund water and sewer lines and road improvements for the new industrial park. "The strongest roots for economic development are formed when local and state leaders work together to provide the resources to create quality jobs," the governor said.

In addition, several groups have joined forces to try to create new industry in the Mississippi Delta region—traditionally the poorest part of Arkansas—as well as in the neighboring states of Mississippi and Louisiana. The W. K. Kellogg Foundation gave a $1.2-million grant to three local universities that are looking for ways to bring new jobs to the region.

Most Arkansas farms are relatively small. The average size is 300 acres. Most of the farmland used for crop production is found in the eastern third of the state, in the Mississippi Delta region, and along the Arkansas River and Red River valleys.

Historically, much of Arkansas's farmwork was done by African Americans who did not own the land they worked on. Since the 1970s, however, farm owners have been employing migrant workers—temporary workers who move throughout the country—to harvest their crops. Many of these workers are from Mexico.

The Arkansas countryside is dotted with the ramshackle cabins of African-American farmworkers who now must compete with migrant workers. In general, Arkansan farm staff work hard for little reward.

EARNING A LIVING

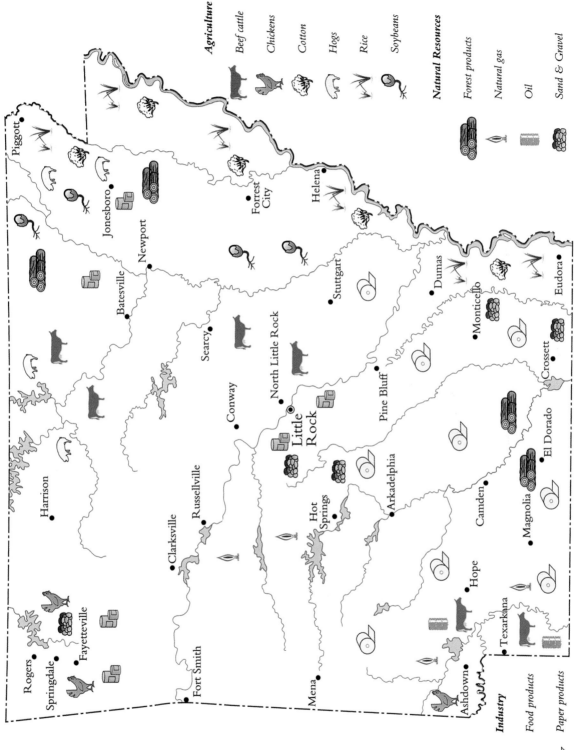

Agriculture

Beef cattle
Chickens
Cotton
Hogs
Rice
Soybeans

Natural Resources

Forest products
Natural gas
Oil
Sand & Gravel

Industry

Food products
Paper products

Piggott
Jonesboro
Newport
Forest City
Helena
Batesville
Stuttgart
Dumas
Monticello
Eudora
Searcy
North Little Rock
Crossett
Conway
Pine Bluff
Little Rock
Arkadelphia
El Dorado
Harrison
Russellville
Hot Springs
Camden
Magnolia
Clarksville
Hope
Rogers
Springdale
Fayetteville
Fort Smith
Mena
Texarkana
Ashdown

"I do whatever they tell me to do—drive the tractor, work with the airplane that sprays the fields, chop the cotton," said one woman. "I do it because I want to work, and I've got to make out the best way I can."

Arkansas leads the nation in the production of rice and is a major producer of soybeans. Recently, a new crop has grabbed farmers' attention—and has begun to fill their fields. The crop is corn, and it is in demand because it can be made into ethanol, a substitute for gasoline. In 2007, Arkansas farmers were expected to grow 500,000 acres of corn, the largest number of acres devoted to this crop in nearly fifty years. Farmers change over from soybeans, cotton, and other crops because corn pays more per acre, and it's relatively easy to convert fields to grow corn.

In addition to crops, livestock plays a major role in Arkansas agriculture, particularly in the northwest. Sixty percent of Arkansas's agricultural income comes from cattle, hogs, eggs, and other livestock products.

Cattle contribute significantly to the state's agricultural income.

Springdale-based Tyson Foods, known for its chicken, is the largest meat-processing company in the world. Its products—chicken, beef, and pork—are sold in more than eighty countries as well as in the United States. In 2005, the company's revenues were reported to be $26 billion. Tyson also plays an active role in the life of the community. In 2007, John Tyson, chairman of the board of Tyson Foods, was named to the board of trustees of the University of Arkansas.

A worker processes chicken parts at a Tyson Foods plant.

The Gulf Coastal Plain of southern Arkansas is the center of a thriving forest-products industry. Union and Columbia counties, near the Louisiana border, are home to a small but prosperous petroleum industry. Other important minerals produced in Arkansas are bromide, natural gas, and coal.

Natural-gas production is expected to surge in Arkansas, thanks to the development of a deposit called the Fayetteville Shale in the state's north-central region. The Arkansas Oil and Gas Commission issued thousands of permits to drill wells. The deposit is deep within the earth, but that has not discouraged exploration. In just six months in 2005, two firms invested $55 million to lease the valuable land and to drill thirty wells.

Much of Arkansas's industry is connected in some way to its wealth of raw materials. The state produces food products, wood products, petro-chemicals, and textiles.

In Des Arc, a worker manufactures kiln-dried hardwood lumber.

DIGGING FOR DIAMONDS

Where in the world can a person just walk into a diamond mine and start digging? There's only one place: the Crater of Diamonds in Murfreesboro, in southwestern Arkansas. Here, in 1906, on a miserable, dusty piece of land, a farmer named John Huddleston was trying to grow crops. He was about to abandon the land when he found a strange, crystalline stone that changed his life. It was a diamond. Huddleston's "worthless" farm sat atop a diamond deposit. At the time it was the only place in the United States known to have diamonds.

Although Huddleston's land was valuable, it was not valuable enough to be turned into a commercial diamond mine. Instead, in 1951, the mine was opened to the public. In 1972, the State of Arkansas bought the land and turned it into a state park. It is the only "finder's-keeper's" diamond mine in the world.

Today, visitors can dig for diamonds to their hearts' content. Visitors can rent digging equipment and listen to a talk on how to prospect. If they're lucky, they'll run into Donald Mayes, the most diligent and successful digger to visit the park. Mayes has dug for diamonds there for thirty years. He generously helps first-timers by showing them how to work the gravel and how to spot a rough diamond.

Over the years, about 75,000 diamonds have been found in the Crater of Diamonds. Most have been small stones, but a few were big enough to name. The 40-carat Uncle Sam, the 16-carat Amarillo Starlight, and the 15-carat Star of Arkansas all were found in the crater. On June 5, 2007, thirteen-year-old Nicole Ruhter of Butler, Missouri, picked up a 2.93-carat diamond along a well-worn path. She named it the Pathfinder Diamond. Eight-year-old twins Grace and Garrett Duncan of Houston, Texas, found a 2.5-carat diamond on a spring-break visit to the park on March 10, 2007.

NEW KINDS OF TOURISTS

In 2005, the Arkansas Tourism Development Act was created to "provide incentives for qualified new or expanding tourism facilities and attractions." The act applies to "cultural or historical sites, recreational or entertainment facilities, areas of natural phenomenon or scenic beauty, theme parks, amusement parks," and more. One of the key factors in the growth of Arkansas's tourism industry is a marketing plan targeted toward visitors from out of state. A casual visit to Arkansas shows that this plan is working. Many of the visitors you will encounter come from neighboring states such as Oklahoma and Missouri.

A family tries its luck digging for diamonds at Crater of Diamonds State Park.

STUDENTS AND BIG CATS

While Arkansas is the natural home of many creatures, it has become a second home to the biggest wild cats in the world: tigers. Tanya and Scott Smith rescue tigers, lions, and other wild animals from people and institutions that can no longer keep them. Their base, just south of Eureka Springs, is called Turpentine Creek Wildlife Rescue. Their land currently contains more than a hundred large mammals. The Smiths nurse the animals back to health and gain their trust. Many of the cats were mistreated by owners of circuses. Others were taken in as babies by people who thought they could raise them as if they were just very large house cats. A 500-pound tiger is no house cat, however, and the "pets" quickly became a problem.

Since 1992, Turpentine Creek has grown into a major rescue park. Young interns do much of the park's work. Most of these college graduates have a science background and a desire to work with wildlife. Spending seven months at the reserve, they learn about the animals and give them all the care and attention they need. In time, most of the animals learn to trust their human caregivers.

A Methodist youth group from nearby Rogers, Arkansas, has made Turpentine Creek its special project. Each year, during spring break, the group helps construct a habitat. This is a wood and wire structure that allows the animals to roam in a natural environment. The group spends four days building a habitat that otherwise would take the staff weeks to build.

It takes a lot of food to satisfy the animals. Arkansas-based Tyson Foods has supplied 95 percent of the reserve's food needs almost from the beginning. Much of the food is frozen chicken, which is fed to the cats in chunks of about 10 to 15 pounds. Wal-Mart recently signed on to provide some red meat as well.

In 2006, tourists spent more than 5 billion dollars in Arkansas. Continued growth in tourism will help Arkansas use its natural beauty and human resources to generate much-needed income. It also will help diversify the state's economy.

IN THE GLOBAL ECONOMY

Arkansas's role in the global economy is significant. In 2006, the state's agricultural exports totaled $1.9 billion, placing Arkansas eleventh among the fifty states. Canada is Arkansas's leading export market. Canada buys 28 percent of all the merchandise exported from Arkansas. Motor vehicle parts were the leading exports to Canada in 2004.

2006 GROSS STATE PRODUCT: $91.8 Million

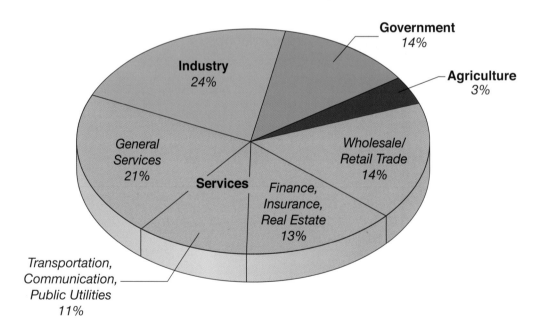

Government
14%

Agriculture
3%

Industry
24%

Wholesale/
Retail Trade
14%

General
Services
21%

Services

Finance,
Insurance,
Real Estate
13%

Transportation,
Communication,
Public Utilities
11%

Other important exports are agricultural products including cereals, dairy products, and honey. Arkansas also exports metals. In addition to shipping goods to Canada, the state sells products to Mexico, Russia, Japan, the United Kingdom, and other countries.

Arkansas also imports goods from Canada. Petroleum is a particularly valuable Canadian import. In addition, Arkansas depends on Canada to meet its energy needs. Imports from Canada totaled $908 million in 2004. This made for an almost perfect balance of trade between Arkansas and its neighbor nation to the north.

Trade agreements have given Arkansas a tremendous boost. Rice, the state's biggest export, gets sold as part of the U.S.-Chile Free Trade Agreement. Chile's import tariff on American rice is set to decrease to zero within about ten years. The opening of the Japanese and Korean markets, as a result of the Uruguay Round of economic talks between 1986 and 1994, also benefited Arkansas exports of rice and poultry. The U.S.-Colombia Trade Promotion Agreement of 2006 has opened the way for major increases in exports to Colombia. American poultry exports to Colombia totaled more than $410 million in 2006.

Chapter Six

The Grand Tour

With its rich history, colorful folklore, and many natural wonders, Arkansas has a wealth of interesting sights. Arkansas's tourism department publishes excellent guides to the state. These yearly guides detail every corner of the state, region by region, and include a section on Arkansas history. There is also a guide devoted to the state's parks, with every single campground listed.

Joe David Rice, tourism director for the Arkansas Department of Parks and Tourism, has worked to develop facilities that attract special kinds of tourists. These cover a wide range of interests. One group is motorcyclists, who find Arkansas's byways and curving back-country roads particularly appealing. Rice also has worked to attract golfers. Five new golf courses with walking trails were developed in Arkansas in 2007. "In our first year, the Arkansas Golf Trail added over $2.15 million to total travel expenditures in our state, and thirty jobs were created," said Rice.

Glory Hole Falls in Newton County is one of countless scenic sights throughout the state.

THE DELTA

We'll start where the first European settlers started in 1686, at Arkansas Post, near where the Arkansas River meets the Mississippi. It was here that Henri de Tonti and his party decided to make a home in the New World.

Today, the place where pioneers first got a foothold in the future state of Arkansas is a national memorial. Nearby, a museum houses artifacts and documents tracing Arkansas history back to colonial times.

This replica of a cross marks Henri de Tonti's 1686 French trading settlement on the Arkansas River.

Moving northward along the Great River Road, which runs alongside the Mississippi, we come to Helena, Arkansas's home of the blues. A restored railroad depot from 1912 houses the Delta Cultural Center, which offers exhibits and educational programs about the history and culture of the region. A featured attraction is a music exhibit that begins with the earliest blues and goes through the rockabilly sound of the 1950s. Another popular spot is Sonny Boy's Music Hall, a picturesque café that features live blues performances.

PLACES TO SEE

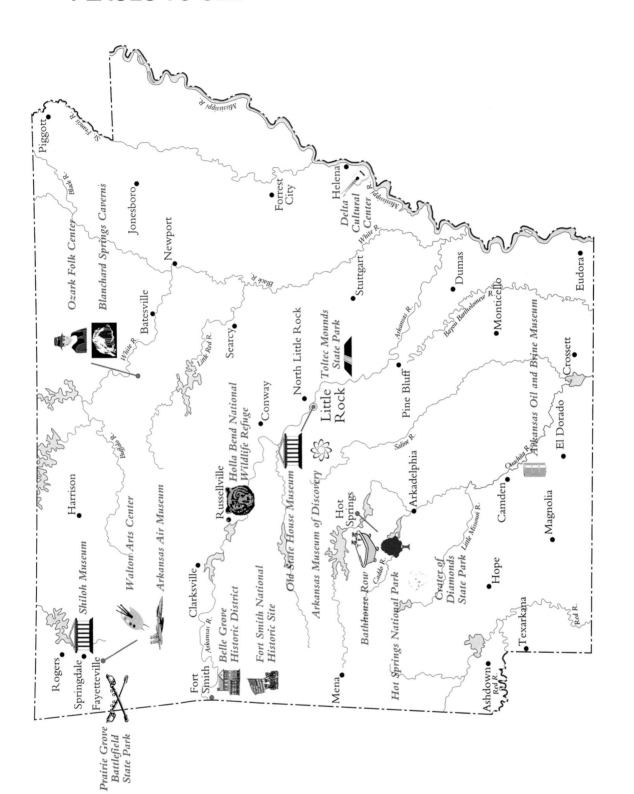

Piggott

St. Francis R.

Mississippi R.

Black R.

Jonesboro

Forrest City

Helena

Delta Cultural Center

Ozark Folk Center

Blanchard Springs Caverns

Newport

Mississippi R.

White R.

Batesville

Black R.

Stuttgart

Dumas

Eudora

Searcy

Little Red R.

White R.

North Little Rock

Toltec Mounds State Park

Arkansas R.

Bayou Bartholomew R.

Monticello

Conway

Little Rock

Pine Bluff

Crossett

Arkansas Oil and Brine Museum

Holla Bend National Wildlife Refuge

Russellville

Buffalo R.

Harrison

Walton Arts Center

Arkansas Air Museum

Old State House Museum

Arkansas Museum of Discovery

Saline R.

Arkadelphia

Ouachita R.

El Dorado

Camden

Magnolia

Shiloh Museum

Clarksville

Hot Springs

Bathhouse Row

Caddo R.

Crater of Diamonds State Park

Little Missouri R.

Hope

Arkansas R.

Belle Grove Historic District

Fort Smith National Historic Site

Rogers

Springdale

Fayetteville

Fort Smith

Mena

Hot Springs National Park

Ashdown

Red R.

Texarkana

Red R.

Prairie Grove Battlefield State Park

THE FASTEST FESTIVAL IN ARKANSAS

Lake Chicot, a genuine Arkansas landmark, is the largest natural oxbow lake in North America. The lake is the perfect setting for the annual U.S. Title Series Hydroplane Races. The race is the featured attraction of the annual Lake Chicot Water Festival. Every year in late June, speedboaters descend on the quiet little town of Lake Village. For those who don't care for boat racing, there's plenty more to see: an acrobatic air show, daredevil bike and skateboard exhibitions, and a fireworks display. People who enjoy quieter pursuits can explore arts and crafts displays, listen to the music of nationally known bands, or attend the always hilarious "beauty pageant" to choose Mr. Lake Chicot.

THE OZARKS

Moving northwest from the delta, we arrive at Powhatan, which has a striking brick courthouse with delicate woodwork. Constructed in 1888, the building served as the seat of Lawrence County's government for almost a hundred years. It is now a museum whose displays reflect life in the eastern Ozarks. A county jail from 1873 and a pre–Civil War log house also have been restored.

Ozark Folk Center State Park in Mountain View is a living museum. It re-creates the folk culture of the mountains. Artisans demonstrate pioneer skills, and musicians perform with old-time folk instruments. The center is both a tourist attraction and a place that preserves a way of life that might otherwise be lost.

Folk musicians perform at Ozark Folk Center State Park in Mountain View.

Northward, near the Missouri line, the Top o' the Ozarks Tower juts skyward from the summit of Bull Mountain. It stands 140 feet tall and is equipped with an elevator for easy access. The structure was built as a lookout, carefully placed to offer the best view of the White River valley below.

Nearby, Mountain Village 1890 is a settlement from the nineteenth century. Visiting the little community, with its authentic buildings and costumed actors, is like stepping through a time warp. Nearby, the Bull Shoals Caverns create their own time-warp effect. In these underground chambers, prehistoric humans found homes, Civil War soldiers found shelter, and moonshiners found a place to hide their illegal whiskey.

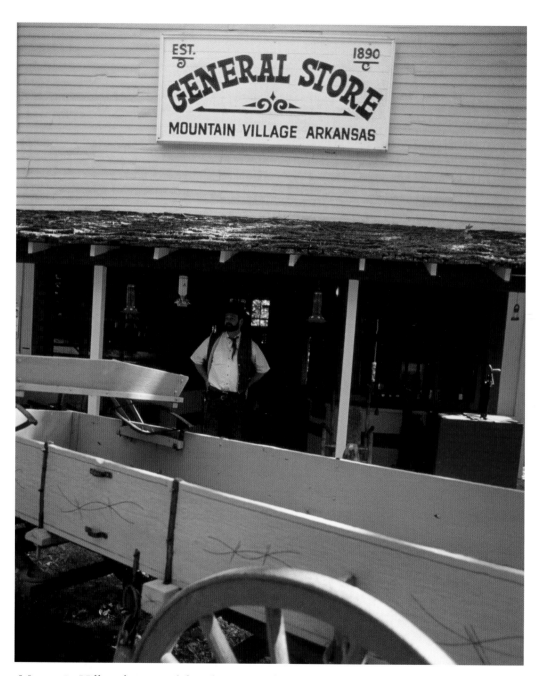

Mountain Village brings to life Arkansas in the nineteenth century.

Farther west, in Eureka Springs, the seven-story Christ of the Ozarks statue overlooks a museum, a memorial chapel, and an amphitheater. The statue depicts Jesus with his arms extended straight out from his shoulders. This makes the figure itself resemble a cross.

In Fayetteville, the Walton Arts Center is an impressive complex of theaters, art galleries, rehearsal studios, and more. The center is home to the North Arkansas Symphony and frequently hosts touring Broadway shows. On the edge of town, the Arkansas Air Museum at Drake Field preserves vintage aircraft, including pre–World War II racing planes that have been restored to flying condition. The museum is headquartered in a historic hangar that dates back to the days when aviation was in its infancy and pilots barnstormed around the country to give exhibitions and rides.

THE WEST AND THE HEARTLAND

Many of Fort Smith's landmarks reflect the city's frontier past. Downtown, the Belle Grove Historic District is a source of pride. It is a twenty-two-block area of restored homes, many of which are more than a hundred years old.

At the Fort Smith National Historic Site, the courtroom of "Hangin' Judge" Isaac Parker is carefully preserved, along with the jail where criminals awaited their appointment with justice. There is also a reproduction of the gallows where many of the criminals met their ends.

In the Belle Grove Historic District of Fort Smith, visitors can tour the John Vaughn House, home of the Fort Smith Art Center.

The neighboring town of Van Buren has transformed its downtown area into what looks like a nineteenth-century shopping district. The people who work in the art galleries, antique shops, and restaurants dress to match the setting—as do some of the tourists who come for a taste of the past. The atmosphere is so authentic that Van Buren's historic downtown has been used for film locations.

Little Rock, in central Arkansas, is the largest city in the state. This state capital has many impressive public buildings. Two of the most notable are the former and present capitol buildings. Construction of the Old State House was begun in 1833 and was finished in 1842. Its Greek Revival style, with graceful columns and clean, classic lines, was popular for public

The Old State House is one of Little Rock's architectural treasures.

buildings of the time. Today, the Old State House is a museum featuring displays such as political memorabilia, African-American quilts, and the inaugural ball gowns of Arkansas's first ladies.

The present statehouse is modeled on the U.S. Capitol in Washington, D.C. Construction began in 1899, but it was 1911 before the legislature could meet in its impressive new chambers. The capitol complex includes a Vietnam War memorial, the Liberty Bell Pavilion, and beautiful gardens that lend an air of southern graciousness to the business of politics.

TEN LARGEST CITIES

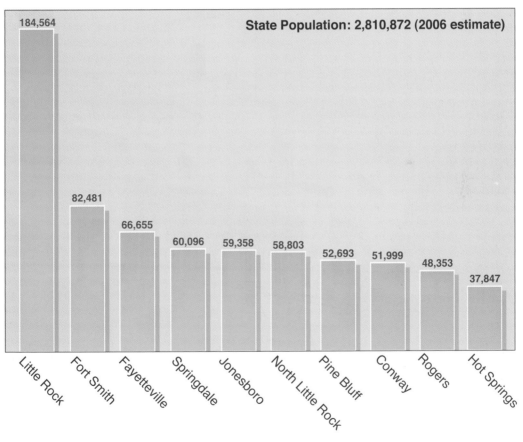

State Population: 2,810,872 (2006 estimate)

City	Population
Little Rock	184,564
Fort Smith	82,481
Fayetteville	66,655
Springdale	60,096
Jonesboro	59,358
North Little Rock	58,803
Pine Bluff	52,693
Conway	51,999
Rogers	48,353
Hot Springs	37,847

THE SOUTHWEST

Moving south into the Ouachitas, we come to the town of Hot Springs, home of the famous mineral waters and a renowned artists' colony. At the heart of Hot Springs is Bathhouse Row, which was named a National Historic Landmark in 1987. Bathhouse Row consists of eight bathhouses built in the early twentieth century. At that time, health consciousness was the latest fad, and people believed that "taking the waters" at mineral hot springs could cure whatever ailed them. Today, only one of the eight bathhouses still functions. Another serves as a visitor center and museum.

Bathhouse Row in Hot Springs National Park is a stately mountain getaway.

The Hot Springs Mountain Tower is a 216-foot observation post atop Hot Springs Mountain. Two viewing levels offer stunning views of Hot Springs National Park and the Ouachita Mountains.

Moving southward into the rolling timberlands, we come to the nineteenth-century town of Washington. The town was established in 1824 and became a regular stop for Texas-bound pioneers. Davy Crockett stopped there, as did Sam Houston and James Bowie. From 1863 to 1865, Washington served as the Confederate capital of Arkansas. Several buildings have been restored or reconstructed, including the capitol building, a tavern, various shops, and several residences.

Closer to the Louisiana border, near the small town of Smackover, three oil derricks mark the Arkansas Museum of Natural Resources. The museum features a working oil well and pumping rig, as well as the three derricks. Inside, exhibits include artifacts and video presentations detailing the history of the 1920s oil boom in southern Arkansas.

Texarkana, the city that straddles two states (Arkansas and Texas) and is named for three (Texas, Arkansas, and Louisiana), makes a good ending point for a tour of Arkansas. One of the town's most popular landmarks is Photographer's Island on State Line Avenue. Here, generations of tourists have posed for snapshots with one foot in Arkansas and the other in Texas. Somehow, this seems fitting in a state that is part Wild West, part Old South, and part hill country.

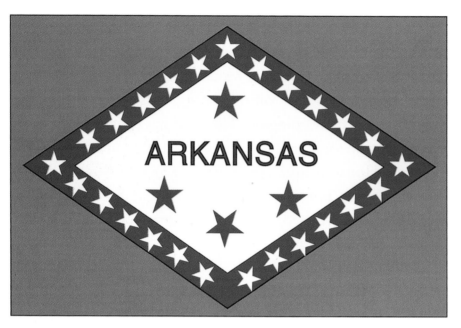

THE FLAG: *Adopted in 1913, the flag is a white diamond on a red field. The twenty-five stars around the diamond indicate that Arkansas was the twenty-fifth state to join the Union. The four stars in the center represent Spain, France, the United States, and the Confederate States of America, the four governments that have ruled Arkansas.*

THE SEAL: *In the seal's center is a shield in front of an American eagle. The shield displays wheat, a steamboat, a beehive, and a plow, which symbolize agricultural and industrial wealth. Above the eagle is the Goddess of Liberty, and to the sides are the Angel of Mercy and the Sword of Justice. The seal was adopted in 1907.*

State Survey

Statehood: June 15, 1836

Origin of Name: From *acansa*, meaning "south wind," a Sioux term for the Quapaw tribe

Nickname: Natural State

Capital: Little Rock

Motto: The People Rule

Bird: Mockingbird

Flower: Apple blossom

Tree: Pine

Insect: Honeybee

Gem: Diamond

Apple blossoms

Honeybee

ARKANSAS (STATE SONG)

"Arkansas" was adopted as the official state song in 1917. It was replaced, then readopted in 1963.

Words and Music by Eva Ware Barnett

GEOGRAPHY

Highest Point: 2,753 feet above sea level, at Magazine Mountain

Lowest Point: 55 feet above sea level, at the Ouachita River in Ashley and Union counties

Area: 53,183 square miles

Greatest Distance North to South: 240 miles

Greatest Distance East to West: 276 miles

Bordering States: Oklahoma and Texas to the west, Missouri to the north, Tennessee and Mississippi to the east, Louisiana to the south

Hottest Recorded Temperature: 120 °F in Ozark on August 10, 1936

Coldest Recorded Temperature: −29 °F in Benton County on February 13, 1905

Average Annual Precipitation: 49 inches

Major Rivers: Arkansas, Black, Mississippi, Ouachita, Red, St. Francis, White

Major Lakes: Beaver, Bull Shoals, Catherine, Chicot, Dardanelle, Felsenthal, Millwood, Norfolk, Ouachita

Trees: ash, basswood, buckeye, dogwood, elm, hickory, holly, locust, maple, oak, pine

Wild Plants: azalea, bluebell, hydrangea, lady's slipper, passionflower, water lily, wild verbena, yellow jasmine

Animals: black bear, bobcat, mink, muskrat, opossum, raccoon, razor-back hog, skunk, weasel, white-tailed deer, woodchuck

Bobcat

Birds: brown thrasher, cardinal, duck, goldfinch, goose, mockingbird, pheasant, phoebe, quail, robin, whippoorwill, wild turkey

Fish: bass, bream, catfish, crappie, perch, pickerel, sturgeon, trout

Endangered Animals: American burying beetle, American peregrine falcon, Arkansas fatmucket, cave crayfish, Curtis' pearly mussel, fat pocketbook, gray bat, Indiana bat, least tern, leopard darter, Magazine Mountain shagreen, Ouachita rock-pocketbook, Ozark big-eared bat, Ozark cavefish, pallid sturgeon, pink mucket pearlymussel, red-cockaded woodpecker, speckled pocketbook

Endangered Plants: eastern prairie fringed orchid, harperella, pondberry, running buffalo clover

TIMELINE

Arkansas History

1500s The Caddo, Osage, and Quapaw tribal groups inhabit the region of modern-day Arkansas.

1541 Hernando de Soto becomes the first European to explore the region.

1673 Father Jacques Marquette and Louis Joliet explore the Mississippi River, including the part in present-day Arkansas.

1682 René-Robert Cavelier, Sieur de La Salle, claims the region for France.

1686 The first European settlement in present-day Arkansas is established in what will become Arkansas Post.

1803 Arkansas becomes a U.S. territory as part of the Louisiana Purchase.

1819 The Arkansas Territory is established with Arkansas Post as its capital; the *Arkansas Gazette*, the state's first newspaper, is established.

1821 The capital moves to Little Rock.

1836 Arkansas becomes the twenty-fifth state.

1843 The Arkansas state legislature establishes a public school system.

1861 The Civil War begins; Arkansas secedes from the Union.

1868 Arkansas is readmitted to the Union.

1871 Arkansas Industrial University, later renamed the University of Arkansas, is founded in Fayetteville.

1874 The present state constitution is adopted.

1887 Bauxite, the main source of aluminum, is discovered near Little Rock.

1888 The state's first free public library is established in Helena.

1906 Diamonds are discovered near Murfreesboro.

1921 Oil is discovered near El Dorado.

1932 Arkansan Hattie Caraway becomes the first woman elected to the U.S. Senate.

1957 Federal troops are sent to help integrate Central High School in Little Rock.

1967 Winthrop Rockefeller becomes the first Republican governor of Arkansas since Reconstruction.

1970 The McClellan-Kerr Arkansas River Navigation System is completed, and large boats can travel all the way across Arkansas to the Mississippi River.

1992 Former Arkansas governor Bill Clinton is elected president of the United States.

1996 Governor Jim Guy Tucker resigns after being convicted of conspiring to defraud financial institutions; President Clinton is reelected.

2004 National Guard brigades from Arkansas are sent to Iraq and Afghanistan.

2006 Mike Beebe is elected governor of Arkansas.

2007 Tornadoes devastate seven Arkansas counties; Mike Huckabee announces he will run for the U.S. presidency.

ECONOMY

Agricultural Products: beef cattle, catfish, chickens, corn, cotton, eggs, hogs, rice, soybeans, tomatoes, wheat

Manufactured Products: airplane parts, chemicals, clothing, electrical equipment, food products, furniture, lumber, paper, steel

Natural Resources: bauxite, bromine, cement, clay, natural gas, oil, sand and gravel, stone, timber

Business and Trade: medical services, tourism, transportation, wholesale and retail trade

CALENDAR OF CELEBRATIONS

Eagle Awareness Weekend Each January outdoor lovers gather in Lakeview to celebrate the bald eagle and other winter wildlife of the Ozarks. Highlights include barge tours to view eagles, guided bird walks, and owl prowls. Visitors also listen to guest speakers and live music.

Jonquil Festival This March festival celebrates the blooming of the jonquils that were planted by some of Hope's earliest settlers. Besides enjoying the fragrance of these lovely flowers, you can hear bluegrass music and watch demonstrations of traditional crafts.

Annual Dulcimer Jamboree The haunting sounds of the dulcimer drift through the Ozark Folk Center in Mountain View during this April event. Musicians come from across the country to participate in workshops and contests. You can also hear performances by previous winners and admire traditional crafts.

Greek Food Festival At this May event in Little Rock, you can feast on luscious Greek and Middle Eastern food, watch Greek dancers, and attend a fashion show.

Riverfest Little Rock bursts to life each May with this celebration of the arts. The festival features ballet, theater, art exhibits, and musical performances to suit every taste. A bike race and a fireworks display add to the fun.

Pink Tomato Festival The highlight of this June event in Warren is an all-tomato luncheon. The menu includes tomato juice, tomato cake, and carrots marinated in tomato soup. The festival also includes a tomato-eating contest, a parade of horse-drawn wagons, a street dance, and a contest for the cutest baby.

Rodeo of the Ozarks In July, Springdale hosts one of the nation's largest outdoor rodeos. At this celebration of cowboy skills, you can see all the traditional events, including bronco riding and calf roping.

Hope Watermelon Festival Watermelons grow to gigantic proportions in Hope—some weigh over 200 pounds. Each August Hope celebrates this fruit with a festival featuring watermelon decorating, eating, and seed-spitting contests. In case visitors get tired of eating watermelon, there are also dancing, music, games, and a big fish fry.

White River Water Carnival This annual event, held at Riverside Park in Batesville, includes arts and crafts, sporting events, a car show, and a parade. It has been held since 1938, when it was started to help people get their minds off the Great Depression.

Ozark Folk Festival Eureka Springs is home to the oldest folk festival west of the Mississippi River. For three days each September, the town bursts with all kinds of folk music. An arts and crafts show brings alive the traditions of the Ozarks.

AutumnFest Each October Fayetteville celebrates the coming of autumn and the fall colors. You can watch parades, dance at the Harvest Ball, or just enjoy lots of delicious food and fun music.

Little Rock Air Force Base Open House During this October open house, thousands of people visit the air force base in Jacksonville to tour airplanes and to watch a thrilling air show.

Arkansas Blues and Heritage Festival (formerly King Biscuit Blues Festival) One of the largest festivals in the South, this celebration in Helena attracts blues fans from around the world each October. Besides listening to great blues and gospel, visitors can stroll among antique and crafts booths, play games, and eat local food.

Arkansas Rice Festival Each October, Weiner celebrates Arkansas's place as the leading rice-producing state. At this festival, you can sample hundreds of rice dishes. Other activities include a cook-off and demonstrations of rice-harvesting machinery.

Wings over the Prairie Festival November is duck season in Stuttgart, and each year tens of thousands of people show up to watch competitors demonstrate their best duck calls. Besides all the quacking, the festival also features the crowning of Queen Mallard, a dance, an arts-and-crafts fair, and a duck gumbo cook-off.

Prairie Grove Battle Reenactment Every other year during the first weekend in December at Prairie Grove Battlefield State Park outside Fayetteville, costumed history buffs reenact this Civil War battle. The event also features a presentation on the life of a Civil War–era soldier.

STATE STARS

Maya Angelou (1928–), an African-American poet, and actress, was born in St. Louis, Missouri, and moved to Stamps, Arkansas, when she was three years old. Angelou is best known for her powerful story of her difficult childhood, *I Know Why the Caged Bird Sings*. Other well-known works include *Just Give Me a Cool Drink of Water 'fore I Diiie* and *All God's Children Need Traveling Shoes*. As an actress, Angelou earned a Tony Award for her role in *Look Away* and an Emmy nomination for her part in the television miniseries *Roots*.

Maya Angelou

Daisy Bates (1920–1999), a civil rights activist, was born in Huttig. In 1941 she and her husband began publishing a newspaper called the *Arkansas State Press*, which attracted many readers by reporting incidents of mistreatment of blacks that other papers ignored. Bates eventually began working with the National Association for the Advancement of Colored People. She became a renowned civil rights leader when she headed the effort to desegregate the Little Rock public schools in 1957. Her book, *The Long Shadow of Little Rock*, details that period in U.S. history.

James Bridges (1936–1993), who was born in Paris, Arkansas, was a film director and screenwriter. Bridges originally set out to be an actor, but after a spell of winning nothing but bit parts, he turned his attention to writing and directing. He became well respected for making entertaining films that also contain strong social commentary. Bridges is best remembered for his films *The Paper Chase* and *The China Syndrome*.

Lou Brock (1939–   ) is considered one of the greatest base stealers in baseball history. Brock began his career with the Chicago Cubs. He was traded to the St. Louis Cardinals in 1964, and he sparked their World Series victory that year. For many years he held the record for the number of career bases stolen—938. Brock, who was born in El Dorado, was inducted into the National Baseball Hall of Fame in 1985.

Lou Brock

Dee Brown (1908–2002) is a historian who wrote *Bury My Heart at Wounded Knee*. This best-selling book discusses the slaughter of Native Americans and the destruction of their culture by the U.S. government in the nineteenth century. Brown was born in Louisiana and moved to Stephens, Arkansas, at age five. He attended Arkansas State Teachers College and eventually became a librarian and professor at the University of Illinois. Brown has written more than twenty books, including *American Spa*, a history of Hot Springs. After retiring from teaching in 1972, Brown returned to Little Rock, Arkansas, to live.

Helen Gurley Brown (1922–   ) was editor in chief of *Cosmopolitan* magazine from 1966 until 1997. When she took over the magazine, it was aimed at housewives. She immediately changed its focus in order to attract what became known as "Cosmo girls"—smart, good-looking, hardworking single women. Brown added lots of material about relationships and emotions and eliminated material about cooking and raising children. By the time she was done, she had transformed *Cosmopolitan* into the remarkably successful Bible of the Unmarried Woman. Brown was born in Green Forest and was raised in Little Rock.

Paul "Bear" Bryant (1913–1983) is one of the most victorious football coaches in history. Born in Moro Bottoms and raised in Fordyce, Bryant earned his nickname when, as a youth, he wrestled a bear. He played college football, became an assistant coach right after graduation, and landed his first head-coaching assignment at the University of Maryland in 1945. He eventually became head coach at the

University of Alabama in 1958 and remained there until he retired in 1982. By that time, he had chalked up 323 victories and six national championships.

Sarah Caldwell (1924–2006), a renowned opera conductor, was raised in Fayetteville. A gifted child, Caldwell was giving violin recitals before age ten and graduated from high school at fourteen. She founded the Opera Company of Boston in 1958 and brought it to national prominence with imaginative productions. In 1976, Caldwell became the first woman to conduct at New York's Metropolitan Opera.

Glen Campbell (1938–   ), who was born in Delight, is a popular country singer and songwriter. His best-known songs include "By the Time I Get to Phoenix," "Wichita Lineman," and "Rhinestone Cowboy." Campbell hosted his own television variety show in the late 1960s and early 1970s.

Hattie Caraway (1878–1950), the first woman ever elected to the U.S. Senate, grew up in Tennessee. She met Thaddeus Caraway in college, and they soon married and settled in Jonesboro, Arkansas. Thaddeus eventually became a U.S. senator. After he died in 1931, Caraway was appointed to complete his term. The following year, she ran for the seat herself and won. During her career, Caraway also became the first woman to preside over a session of the Senate, the first woman Senate committee chairperson, and the first woman to conduct a Senate committee hearing. Caraway served in the Senate until 1945.

Johnny Cash (1932–2003), whose deep growl of a voice is known worldwide, was a giant in country music. Cash grew up poor in the town of Kingsland. In the 1950s, he taught himself to play guitar, moved to Memphis, Tennessee, and began performing and recording country and rockabilly songs. Many of his hits from this era, including "I Walk the Line" and "Folsom Prison Blues," have become classics. Cash has been inducted into both the Rock and Roll and Country Music halls of fame.

Johnny Cash

Bill Clinton (1946–   ), the forty-second president of the United States, was born in Hope and grew up in Hot Springs. An excellent student, Clinton became a lawyer and began teaching law at the University of Arkansas. He soon became Arkansas's attorney general and, in 1978, was elected the youngest governor in the state's history. He served four full terms as governor before being elected president in 1992. Clinton was reelected in 1996. After he left the presidency, he set up the William J. Clinton Foundation, whose mission is to use the planet's resources for the benefit of poor people everywhere.

Bill Clinton

Dizzy Dean (1911–1974), who was born in Lucas, was a legendary baseball pitcher. Dean took Major League Baseball by storm in 1932, his first full season, by winning eighteen games. Two years later, he won thirty games—a record that would stand for thirty-four years—and led the St. Louis Cardinals to a World Series victory. By the time his career was cut short by injury, Dean had won 150 games. He was elected to the National Baseball Hall of Fame in 1953.

J. William Fulbright (1905–1995), a U.S. senator, was the force behind the prestigious Fulbright Program. Fulbright grew up in Fayetteville, attended the University of Arkansas, and, in 1943, began serving in the U.S. House of Representatives. He soon moved to the Senate, where he earned a reputation as a champion of international understanding. His greatest legacy is the Fulbright Program, which provides grants for American scholars to do research abroad and for foreign students to study in the United States. Fulbright is also remembered because, in 1966, he became the first prominent member of Congress to criticize the Vietnam War.

Ellen Gilchrist (1935–   ), who lives in Fayetteville, is a well-respected poet and fiction writer. In such books as *In the Land of Dreamy Dreams* and *Falling Through Space*, she provides a candid view of well-to-do Southern society. Her 1984 short-story collection, *Victory over Japan*, won the American Book Award.

Al Green (1946–   ) is a popular soul and gospel singer from Forrest City. Green first hit number one in 1972, with "Let's Stay Together." After a string of hits in the 1970s, Green stopped singing pop music to become a minister and a gospel singer. Green's smooth, silky voice has brought him critical acclaim—he's won nine Grammy Awards—and has made him one of the most successful recording artists of all time.

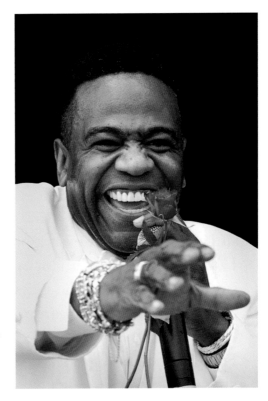

Al Green

John Grisham (1955–   ) is a lawyer who has written a string of best-selling novels about the legal profession. Thirteen of his books, including *The Firm*, *The Pelican Brief*, and *The Client*, have been made into popular movies. Grisham was born in Jonesboro. His output is steady—he writes a book a year—and remarkably successful. More than 225 million copies of his books are in print in twenty-nine languages.

John H. Johnson (1918–2005) was the head of the most powerful African-American publishing company in the United States. In 1942, he founded *Negro Digest*, a magazine that included articles of interest to African Americans from other newspapers and magazines. After *Negro Digest* quickly attracted a large readership, Johnson also founded *Ebony* and *Jet* magazines. Johnson was born in Arkansas City.

Scott Joplin (1868–1917), an African-American composer from Texarkana, is known as the King of Ragtime. Joplin popularized ragtime music, which is noted for its strong rhythms and lively, intricate melodies. His "Maple Leaf Rag" was the most popular ragtime song at the turn of the century—millions of copies of the sheet music were sold. Today, Joplin is best known for his song "The Entertainer," which earned wide popularity after it was used in the 1973 movie *The Sting*.

Alan Ladd (1913–1964) was a popular actor of the 1940s and 1950s. Ladd, who was born in Hot Springs, began his career performing small roles in movies and plays. His big break came when he was cast in the starring role as a paid killer in *This Gun for Hire*. From then on he appeared in film after film as a quiet tough guy. His most famous role was the mysterious stranger in the classic Western *Shane*.

Douglas MacArthur

Douglas MacArthur (1880–1964), one of the most celebrated military generals of the twentieth century, was born in Little Rock. He attended the United States Military Academy at West Point, where he graduated first in his class, and then worked his way up through the U.S. Army ranks to become a five-star general. During World War II, MacArthur became the supreme commander of Allied forces in the Pacific. He led United Nations forces during the Korean War until a conflict with President Harry Truman over whether to extend the war into China led to his dismissal.

Patsy Montana (1914–1996) of Hot Springs was the first major female star in country music. With her cowgirl image and her fantastic yodeling, she shot up the charts in 1935 with her hit "I Want to Be a Cowboy's Sweetheart." This was the first single by a female country singer to sell more than a million copies.

Scottie Pippen (1965–   ) was a starting guard with the Chicago Bulls. During Pippen's time with the Bulls, the team won the National Basketball Association (NBA) championship six times. Pippen was born in Hamburg, and he played college ball at the University of Central Arkansas. Pippen entered the NBA in 1987, became a starter for the Bulls in 1988, and was an NBA All-Star every year from 1990 until his retirement in 2004. In 1996, the NBA named Pippen one of the fifty greatest players of all time.

Scottie Pippen

Brooks Robinson (1937–   ), a Little Rock native, is considered by many to be the greatest third baseman in the history of baseball. Robinson began playing for the Baltimore Orioles in 1955, and his outstanding fielding soon earned him acclaim. During his twenty-two years with the Orioles, his consistent defensive work earned him sixteen Golden Glove Awards, a record he shares with Jim Kaat and Greg Maddux. Robinson was elected to the National Baseball Hall of Fame in 1983.

Mary Steenburgen (1953–   ) is an Academy Award–winning actress who grew up in North Little Rock. Steenburgen made her movie debut opposite Jack Nicholson in the 1978 film *Goin' South*. Starring in such films as *Ragtime*, *Time After Time*, and *Parenthood*, she quickly established a reputation for playing characters who are soft-spoken, a bit eccentric, and often very determined. In 1981 she won the Academy Award for Best Supporting Actress for her role in *Melvin and Howard*. In 2006, Steenburgen received an honorary doctor of humane letters degree from Lyon College in Batesville.

William Grant Still (1895–1978) was a violinist and a groundbreaking composer. Still was born in Mississippi and grew up in Little Rock. He played violin as a child but did not seriously consider music as a career until college. He eventually moved to New York City, where he began incorporating jazz and folk tunes into his compositions. In 1931, his *Afro-American Symphony* became the first symphony by a black American to be performed by a major orchestra. Still was also the first African American to conduct a major symphony orchestra and to compose an opera performed by a major company.

Edward Durell Stone (1902–1978) was a renowned architect who helped change the face of New York City. Born in Fayetteville, Stone studied at the University of Arkansas before embarking on his career. He helped design Radio City Music Hall, the Museum of Modern Art, and the General Motors building, all in New York City. He also worked on the U.S. embassy building in New Delhi, India. Stone's designs were often controversial. In his later years he criticized people who tore down old buildings with no concern for their historical importance.

Barry Switzer (1937–) was born in Crossett. As head coach of the Dallas Cowboys, he led the team to a Super Bowl championship following the 1995 season. Switzer played college football at the University of Arkansas and later gained fame coaching at the University of Oklahoma, where he led his team to three national championships. Switzer was elected to the College Football Hall of Fame in 2002, and he received the Jim Thorpe Lifetime Achievement Award in 2004.

Sam Walton (1918–1992), who founded the Wal-Mart chain of stores, was the richest man in the United States for several years. Walton grew up in Missouri and began working in discount stores after graduating from college. Most discount chains had stores only in cities. Walton believed the chains shouldn't ignore the huge market of smaller towns and suburbs. In 1962, he opened the first Wal-Mart in Rogers, Arkansas. His idea quickly took off. By the time Walton died, more than 1,700 Wal-Marts were spread across the country.

TOUR THE STATE

Arkansas Territorial Restoration (Little Rock) Four restored homes from the early nineteenth century give visitors a taste of frontier life.

Big Dam Bridge (Little Rock) This bridge, which spans the Murray Lock, was dedicated in September 2006. It is the world's longest (3,463 feet) pedestrian and bicycle bridge built for this purpose. The bridge connects biking and hiking trails in the cities of Little Rock and North Little Rock.

Crystal Bridges Museum of American Art (Bentonville) Founded by Alice Walton, wife of Sam Walton, this museum showcases American heritage through its artworks.

Old State House Museum (Little Rock) The Old State House, which opened in 1836, is now a historical museum, where you can visit the restored legislative meeting rooms and governor's office. Another room is filled with hands-on exhibits, such as old clothing that can be tried on and tools of everyday life you can handle.

Arkansas Museum of Discovery (Little Rock) At this museum, visitors can build a robot, experiment with magnets, and construct a tepee. It is a great place to spend a day with children.

Toltec Mounds Archaeological State Park (England) This was once the site of one of the largest Native-American settlements in the region. Today, you can see the remnants of some of the mounds that were built between 700 and 950 CE.

Blanchard Springs Caverns (Mountain View) A tour of these spectacular caverns takes you past extraordinary cave formations and along a glistening cave stream.

Blanchard Springs Caverns

Ozark Folk Center (Mountain View) This center is dedicated to preserving traditional Ozark culture. People dressed in period clothes demonstrate traditional crafts such as candle making, pottery, basketry, broom and doll making, and musical instruments. Visitors can purchase items that the craftspeople make. Special programs for children introduce them to crafting. Musicians perform mountain music outdoors or in the center's auditorium.

Holla Bend National Wildlife Refuge (Dardanelle) Bald eagles, herons, egrets, sandpipers, ducks, and geese all make this wildlife refuge their winter home.

Crater of Diamonds State Park (Murfreesboro) The spot where a lucky farmer once uncovered a diamond is now a park where anyone can hunt for them. Visitors have found about 75,000 diamonds so far.

Eureka Springs (Eureka Springs) This quaint nineteenth-century town is tucked into a mountainside. Droves of visitors wander the narrow streets and browse in the charming shops.

Arkansas Air Museum (Fayetteville) Housed in an old wooden hangar, this museum features antique airplanes and exhibits about the history of aviation.

Hot Springs National Park (Hot Springs) At this popular resort area, water comes out of the ground at 143 °F. The park is home to several historic bathhouses that were built in the early twentieth century, when people went to Hot Springs because they thought its water had healing powers. Today, in addition to taking a soak in the waters, visitors can hike to the Hot Springs Mountain Tower, which offers a spectacular view of the Ouachita Mountains.

Fort Smith National Historic Site (Fort Smith) One of the first U.S. military posts in the Louisiana Territory, this site offers a taste of the Old West. You can tour the courtroom where Judge Isaac Parker, the Hangin' Judge, presided and view the jail in which prisoners were held.

Shiloh Museum of Ozark History (Springdale) This excellent museum is devoted to preserving the history of northwestern Arkansas. Several historic buildings from the nineteenth century, including a log cabin, a doctor's office, and a post office, have been moved to the site. Displays also feature antique photographs, farm equipment, and Native-American artifacts.

Prairie Grove Battlefield State Park (Prairie Grove) On December 7, 1862, Confederate and Union forces clashed at this site in a bloody battle. Today, the park features exhibits that bring the world of a Civil War soldier to life. You can also visit reconstructed nineteenth-century buildings.

Buffalo National River (Harrison) Canoeists and rafters love traveling down this river, past towering cliffs and majestic canyons. They can also camp, fish, and hike.

Delta Cultural Center (Helena) At this museum, which is housed in a 1912 train depot, you can learn everything about the delta, from the roots of the delta blues to how frequent flooding devastated pioneer farmers.

FUN FACTS

The city of Texarkana straddles the Arkansas-Texas border. It has two city governments, one for each side, but the post office sits exactly on the line between the two states. The building is constructed of half Texas granite and half Arkansas limestone. Its address is Texarkana, Arkansas-Texas.

Hope, Arkansas, is the home of the world record for the heaviest watermelon. The largest watermelon ever entered into the town's annual 4-H contest weighed in officially at 130 pounds.

It is illegal for dogs to bark after 6:00 P.M. in Fayetteville.

It is legal to shoot a bear in Arkansas, but it is illegal to wake a bear up in order to take its picture.

The town of Hector, Arkansas, was named after President Grover Cleveland's dog.

Find Out More

If you would like to find out more about Arkansas, look in your school library, local library, bookstore, or video store. You can also surf the Internet. Here are some resources to help you begin your search.

BOOKS

Baker, T. Harri and Jane Browning. *Arkansas History for Young People.* Fayetteville: University of Arkansas Press, 2007.

King, David C. *Arkansas.* New York: Benchmark Books, 2007.

Lantier, Patricia. *Arkansas.* Strongsville, OH: Gareth Stevens, 2005.

Marsh, Carole. *Arkansas Symbols & Facts Projects: 30 Cool Activities, Crafts, Experiments & More for Kids to Do to Learn About Your State.* Peachtree City, GA: Gallopade International, 2003.

VIDEOS

Off to War: From Rural Arkansas to Iraq. Kino Videos, 2005. This video follows an Arkansas National Guard brigade as it makes the transition from "weekend warriors" to a fighting unit in Iraq.

Rivers of North America: Arkansas River. Film Ideas, 2006. This video looks at the role that the Arkansas River plays in the life of the state.

WEB SITES

The Encyclopedia of Arkansas History & Culture

http://encyclopediaofarkansas.net

This is one of the best online sources of information about everything that is, was, or will be Arkansas. It's perfect for report writing or browsing for fun facts.

Clinton Presidential Center

www.clintonpresidentialcenter.org

Interactive displays allow visitors to walk through a timeline of Clinton's accomplishments.

Arkansas.gov

www.arkansas.gov

This is the official Web site of the State of Arkansas. It includes facts about the state and its history, its tourism and business activities, and its government offices.

The Department of Arkansas Heritage

http://www.arkansasheritage.com

Learn about Arkansas's many cultures and their histories.

King Biscuit Time Radio

http://www.kingbiscuittime.com/radio.html

Visitors to this site can listen to the daily broadcast of the famous music and talk program from the heart of the Ozarks.

Index

Page numbers in **boldface** are illustrations and charts.

ABOUT THE AUTHOR

Linda Jacobs Altman has written many books for young people, including *California* in the Celebrate the States series. She lives in Clearlake, California, with her husband and an assortment of four-legged friends. Her son and two grandchildren live in Arkansas.

Ettagale Blauer and Jason Lauré traveled the length and breadth of Arkansas to research this book. They explored the towns and natural landscapes. They visited the Crater of Diamonds in Murfreesboro, marveled at the tigers at Turpentine Creek Wildlife Rescue, and listened to the "pickers" play folk music in Mountain View. They drove around the amazing town of Eureka Springs, where it feels as if you've gone back a hundred years in time. All over the state they found Southern hospitality flourishing. The beauty of Arkansas was a delightful surprise. Blauer and Lauré have written thirty books for young adults.